MW01114872

Value Prop
Misperception in Decision Making

Neil Rackham. Author: *Spin Selling.* "Books in the field of persuasion and influence are usually disappointing. It's an area where you mostly find a little thought and a whole lot of hype. Rick Dove's book is an exception. It is thoughtful, closely argued, and makes you think. Any professional interested in selling and persuading will find this book worthwhile and rewarding."

Joel Orr, Vice President, Cyon Research. Author: *The Victorious Engineer.* "'Everybody is in sales' is a provocative phrase, repeated for the last several decades throughout the corporate world. At the same time, sales is often identified with persuasion, coercion, deception, and seduction. Yet sales, I've become convinced, is at the heart of win-win business and professional activities. It involves helping people see the wisdom of buying. … I cannot think of a category of people who will not gain immensely by reading Rick Dove's book and studying its recommendations. It derives from a profound understanding of human learning and decision making, simultaneously analytical and intuitive. This approach is a powerful tool for good. You owe it to yourself to read Rick's book."

Greg Lefelar, Manager, Federal eServer Sales, IBM. "I found this book very insightful on the forces in action within any business interaction. Rick provides a technical, yet very commonsense approach in describing influencers and decision makers and the variables which affect how decision makers ultimately decide. *Value Propositioning* can be a valuable educational tool for sales professionals in understanding the tremendous importance of building trust with their clients, and in building competency with their brand. Rick delivers his work with the experience of someone who has obviously 'been there' and with a subtle sense of humor that makes it an enjoyable read."

Value
Propositioning

Value Propositioning

Book One

Perception and Misperception in Decision Making

Rick Dove

Value Propositioning
Book One: Perception and Misperception in Decision Making

Published by Iceni Books®
610 East Delano Street, Suite 104
Tucson, Arizona 85705 U.S.A.
www.icenibooks.com

Cover illustration by Maureen Burdock.

International Standard Book Number: 1-58736-389-5
Library of Congress Control Number: 2004111782

This book is dedicated to the people who have, in one way or another, inspired its creation. They are: Bob Abbott, Becky Bace, Steve Benson, Joan Bigham, John Boardman, Steve Della Rochetta, Cece Dove, Melanie Graham, Cy Hannon, Bill Herington, Howard Kuhn, Charanjit Lohara, Pat Maley, Niccolo Machiavelli, Ray Pawlawski, Jack Ring, Larry Rhoades, Mike Ronayne, Mike Rynerson, Sergio Sperat, Dave Tilstone, and Ray Zara. Many of them will wonder at this.

Contents

Part 1

Concepts That Form the Core of
Value Propositioning

Part 2

Logic That Structures Core Concepts
and Drives Decision Making

Acknowledgements

This book started out as a personal reflection and sense making of observation and experience. To my delight and encouragement, it gained legitimacy, at least in my mind, from the seminal thinking and research of Richard Cyert, Daniel Kahneman, James March, Herb Simon, and Amos Tversky. Their work on the psychology of decision-making behavior and bounded rationality grounded what would have otherwise relied upon anecdotal opinion. I am also indebted to Scott Plous for his published interpretations of this body of work. My use of the knowledge developed by these men is focused somewhat differently than what they had in mind. Though I have attempted to represent their conclusions accurately, I have necessarily extended the application of their thinking specifically to the activities involved in value propositioning.

Both Joseph Novak's work on concept maps and David Ausubel's on learning theory have had profound personal effects, as well as obvious utility in the graphic representation of each chapter's material. Concept maps were an invaluable tool in distilling the previously mentioned work of behavioral decision making, and became equally invaluable in converting personal tacit knowledge into cogent explicit knowledge. Ausubel's maxim, that effective knowledge transfer is an incremental excursion from what is already known, lent discipline to the progression of presentation and legitimacy to what I've long suspected as necessary.

Jack Ring suggested that Novak's concept maps would help me organize and present my thoughts. He was more than right. In so doing, he transformed my writing experience into a deeply rewarding learning experience.

Bob Dove, educator and schooled journalist that he is, waded through yet another manuscript critique, as only a brother would.

Thoughtful and critical encouragement during any book project is invaluable. For that I thank Steve Benson, Joan Bigham, Larry Dorie, Bob Dove, Steve Goldman, Melanie Graham, Greg Lefelar, Joel Orr, Jack Ring, David Ulman, and Bill White.

Introduction

I spent the nineties investigating the physics of agile enterprise, focused on organizational architectures that enable rapid change on any dimension. I came to know that this ability to respond is only one key aspect of enterprise agility. Knowledge of what requires a response is the second key aspect, and deciding how to respond is the third. I have since come to respect the difficulties associated with making that decision effectively.

Value propositioning happens in all conversations that attempt to obtain a favorable decision among alternatives. Sometimes it is done by the Decision Champion, who seeks the decision. Sometimes it is done by the Decision Maker, who seeks an understanding. Regardless of whether one or both do it, three factors get in the way: human...decision-making...behavior.

This book is about how business decisions are really made. It focuses on what really happens, how it really happens, and why it really happens. It does not, like so many new books every year, provide yet another analytical procedure for making optimal selections among alternatives. It illuminates something much more fundamental: Decisions are always made in favor of the choice with the best value—*as perceived by the Decision Maker*. Perception is everything, but perceptions are formed independent of truth, accuracy, and the best intentions of all parties.

In many respects, perceptions are like reflections. They mirror the knowledge, behavior, and psychology of the decision maker. It is the way we are wired.

For sure, this behind-the-looking-glass knowledge will lead to better decisions—not because it provides a new scoring mechanism for sorting amongst alternatives, but because it focuses on the nature of value perception and misperception. Decisions are made by people, whether as sole deciders or as members of a decision-making coalition. No two people perceive the same thing in exactly the same way, whether it is the problem to be solved, candidate solutions, value priorities, or even the importance of a decision.

On the surface, this book speaks directly to Decision Champions, as opposed to Decision Makers. A Decision Champion is that person seeking a favorable decision, and therefore is responsible for making an effective value proposition. I cast the Champion as the active party and the Decision Maker as the passive party. Not because this always is, or should be, the case, but rather because the Champion is typically in competition to show better value than all other acceptable alternatives. I am tempted to say that the Champion therefore has more to lose if value is not perceived in its best light. But of course this is not true—all parties have a lot to lose.

Champions take on a cause, leading the charge for respect and approval, where causes are projects, purchases, strategies, capital expenditures, or whatever competes for corporate priority and resource. The focus here is on causes of enterprise magnitude, where decision choices have broad implications, and on technology-based causes, which bring special dimensions of confusion and complexity.

The Champion wields a value proposition in competition for approval, much like the Knight wields a sword defending a Lady's honor. The Knight engages in sword play; the Champion engages in value propositioning. In the Knight's competition, the quality of the sword and the quality of the competitor are two independent factors. So it is with the Champion's competition.

My approach is pragmatic and blunt. It recognizes that Champions appeal to Decision Makers for approval. Approval is the goal. Decision Makers bestow goal-dom. Ergo! A Champion's focus needs to be on the Decision Maker and how decisions are reached, rather than on the righteousness of the thing being championed. This understanding is especially lacking when technology is being championed, as both Champion and Decision Maker are variously seduced, overwhelmed, impressed, humbled, lost, confused, trusting, skeptical, repulsed, and infatuated when technology is the issue.

Where technology projects or products are concerned, I find too often no acceptance of responsibility for crafting effective value propositions. There seems instead a belief that technology stands naked for all to see and evaluate, needing only a guided tour of features and obvious benefits, and that an inappropriate evaluation is a fault of the evaluator and not of the Champion. I hope to change this, and will show that an effective value proposition is not about the technology (the solution), but rather about the problem and value perceptions of the people who will choose a solution.

I have sensed for some time that decisions are not based on the surface issues that people argue and evaluate. Similarly, I've known that return-on-investment is not the positive decision factor it's cracked up to be, but rather a gate to pass through, and not much more than a formality at that, and that price and cost savings are much overrated as decision factors. Perhaps you have some of this same tacit knowledge. Not until writing this book, however, have I attempted to articulate consciously and comprehensively what is really going on, and to find out what others think and know. To my surprise, I found documented validity and respected theory based on decades of learned research about decision making. This discussion, however, is based on common sense, rather than expounding the academic theory and research that supports it, though some will peek through when necessary. For those interested, I've provided references to the relevant academic work at the very end.

My perceptions have been shaped by a career of start-up ventures, turnarounds, and change management. I learned early that with impatience the venture capitalist will interrupt you before ten minutes is up and demand, "What is the value proposition?" And you shouldn't come back until you can articulate that clearly. In this context, the value proposition stems from innovative features that provide preemptive benefits to a defined market. This value proposition must be articulated by every company that addresses a competitive market with some service or product. Development people proposing a new innovative product learn this. Marketing people trying to differentiate their company learn this. Sales people trying to explain their product learn this. What they all learn has set them off in the wrong direction for making good value propositions to Decision Makers. The difference is that value propositions which justify products in markets are static general statements, whereas value propositions that influence a specific Decision Maker must be custom fit to that Decision Maker's situation, done so in real time, and redone continuously as the Decision Maker's perceptions evolve.

The thing a Champion must accomplish is to win approval from those who control corporate priorities and strategy, those who commit funds and resources. This may mean an engineering project manager winning approval for an internal development project, an account manager seeking selection as an external supplier of products or services, or a business manager seeking budget, capital, or strategy approval. In all cases the process is fundamentally the same. In this respect we see that some key responsibilities and skills of technically-focused people, business-focused people, and sales-focused people are identical (we pause while all parties shudder at this repulsive thought). They are all successful only to the extent that they can be effective Champions of the projects and products they want Decision Makers to value and select. When they play the role of the Champion effectively, they are indistinguishable. All face the same Decision Makers employing the same decision logic, and all win with the same skills, perspective, and argument strategy.

The second book in this series is currently in process, and addresses the personal development of a Champion's competency and talent at value propositioning, consistent with the fundamentals contained in Book One. Book Three will address the same for the Decision Maker; though value propositioning is a game played between Champion and Decision Maker, it has a win-win or lose-lose outcome.

Book One, under your eyes now, is organized in two parts. The first lays groundwork by introducing fundamental concepts, and the second shows how these concepts relate to each other, coalescing as behavioral models of decision-making logic and knowledge development. You will develop insight based on common sense and cause-and-effect models that reflect the way decisions are really made, instead of the way popular advice suggests they ought to be. You will understand how things work like few others do. This understanding will have an immediate effect on your appreciation and approach to the process of value propositioning and decision making.

And since I know that many people have already written about these matters, I fear that I shall be considered presumptuous in writing about them, too, the more so because in treating this subject I depart from the rules set down by others. But since it is my intention to write something of use to those who will understand, I deem it best to stick to the practical truth of things rather than to fancies. [Niccolo Machiavelli, *The Prince*, Chapter 15, as translated by Daniel Donno, Bantam Classic reissue, 2003.]

A Special Note about the Graphics

Every section of this book includes a graphic called a *concept map*. This is a particularly useful and clear representation of knowledge that Joseph Novak (see references section) developed and trademarked. Concept maps visually summarize the central ideas and their relationships in each section. They have a surprising ability to clarify the densest, information-packed text, and to show on one page what takes many pages to explain in words. They don't usually convey full meaning, however, until after the text is first read, as they are somewhat like an outline. Concept maps follow simple rules: they are hierarchical, in that concepts lower in the diagram are refinements of concepts higher in the diagram; relationships are directed downward along connecting lines, as befits a hierarchy, unless an arrowhead is present to show differently; and one should be able to clearly read a meaningful thought when traversing connected concepts.

Part 1

Concepts That Form the Core of Value Propositioning

1

On the Nature of Value and Value Propositions

A value proposition is an instrument that a Champion employs to influence Decision Makers. In its elemental form, a value proposition is an itemization of features and their benefits, relevant to a proposed solution for a specific problem. In these respects a value proposition is in competition to establish superior worth in the context of the problem. The value proposition attempts to say: "Here is why you should rule in favor of this proposal over all others."

A comprehensive value proposition generally presents multiple benefits, each expected to convey value of some kind and some amount. Typically the features and benefits from one choice alternative to another are not a one-to-one match, as Champions try to differentiate their solutions. To enable comparison, the Decision Maker employs a common metric I'll call Value (with a capital V), and a method to reduce multiple value dimensions and measures into this single metric.

This Value is therefore the composite judgment assigned to something in order to make a decision among alternatives. In this general process, all benefits deemed relevant by a Decision Maker are assigned a relative weighting, whether overt and explicit or unstated and intuitive. The relevant benefits from a specific alternative are assigned values, which are then factored by the weightings, and the sum of all weighted values reduces to this single Value measure, which is comparable across alternatives. This process is personal and subjective, and not to be confused with some subsequent formal methodology employed as an overt and seemingly objective way to arrive at a composite judgment.

There is argument about how best to mathematically reduce judgments of multiple individual benefits into a single Value. These arguments are generally about alternative mathematical or logical models and their appropriateness. Arguments of this nature provide interesting analytical debate, but have little to do with the reality of decision making, which is typically arrived at subjectively, and then justified with a compatible mathematical model or logical argument.

Higher Value is what decision makers seek, and higher Value is what determines the decision among alternatives. People do not make a decision in favor of a lower Value alternative. This is unequivocal, and might seem unnecessary to say, but Value is a personal judgment assigned by an individual, and so there is no concept of accuracy associated with it. One individual's Value is not necessarily equal to another's, and decision making, as it is actually practiced, is not typically an optimizing, objective act.

A simple example will serve for now. A commodity is an item undifferentiated from others like it in feature and quality. Comparing Value among commodity alternatives would seem a simple matter of comparing costs. Judgment, implying a subjective evaluation, would seem out of place. But then, why do many people choose a national brand cold remedy when next to it at the discount store is a house brand at one-fifth the cost (yes, really), with identical ingredients, alike in all respects but name and packaging art, neither of which affects medical effectiveness? A composite judgment is a weighted roll-up of multiple benefit values, with a weighting and judgment made for each individual benefit. Deciding which cold remedy to purchase may, for different people, include perceived benefits of brand image (more doctors recommend it), or personal image (I don't buy cheap stuff), or tradition (I grew up with this), or perceived risk (it might be more pure), or prior satisfaction (it worked last time), or even nonsense (it works faster).

Value judgments can range from objective to subjective. The initial cost, for instance, of committing to a particular technology acquisition or development project is usually a known number (objective), whereas its true cost of ownership or pursuit over time is a conjecture of future events (mix of objective with subjective), while the envisioned experience of ownership is individually per-

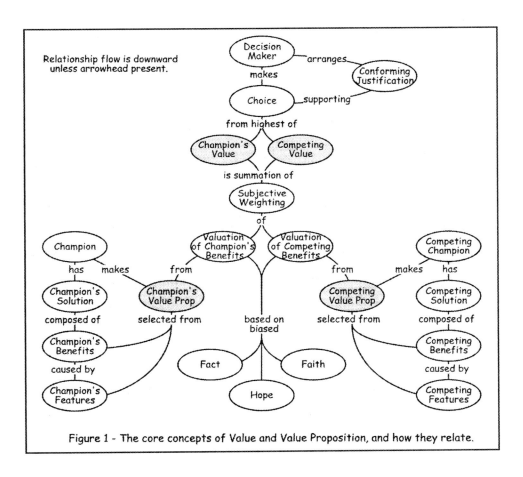

Relationship flow is downward unless arrowhead present.

Decision Maker —arranges→ Conforming Justification

Decision Maker —makes→ Choice

Choice —supporting→ Conforming Justification

Choice —from highest of→ Champion's Value / Competing Value

is summation of

Subjective Weighting

of

Valuation of Champion's Benefits / Valuation of Competing Benefits

Champion —has→ Champion's Solution
Champion —makes→ Champion's Value Prop

Valuation of Champion's Benefits —from→ Champion's Value Prop

Champion's Solution —composed of→ Champion's Benefits

Champion's Value Prop —selected from→ Champion's Benefits

Champion's Benefits —caused by→ Champion's Features

Champion's Features —selected from→ Champion's Value Prop

based on biased

Fact   Faith

Hope

Competing Champion —has→ Competing Solution
Competing Champion —makes→ Competing Value Prop

Valuation of Competing Benefits —from→ Competing Value Prop

Competing Solution —composed of→ Competing Benefits

Competing Value Prop —selected from→ Competing Benefits

Competing Benefits —caused by→ Competing Features

Figure 1 - The core concepts of Value and Value Proposition, and how they relate.

sonal and emotional (subjective). These three bases for judgment can be characterized as fact, hope, and faith.

Though one may wish for an objective evaluation of benefits, and a predictable process for arriving at a composite Value for a total proposition, this is generally not the case. The effective Champion understands that value judgments can be biased, borrowed, whimsical, coerced, and subject to change without notice, and therefore that Champion pursues a value-propositioning strategy that addresses the behavioral logic of decision making. These behavioral aspects will be examined later in some depth.

2

On the Nature of Decision Makers and Champions

A Decision Maker chooses the best fit for a perceived problem among candidate solutions. A Champion is the advocate for a particular solution, and attempts to create a perception of superior value in the mind of the Decision Maker.

Though there are cases where decisions for a solution to a significant enterprise problem are the responsibility of a single person, usually such decisions are made by a coalition of participants. Meaningful participants are those affected by the problem and those who will be affected by the solution. Typically these are representatives chosen from multiple divisions, departments, and suborganizations within the enterprise. For instance, a project that requires capital funds might be evaluated by a capital expenditures committee with representatives from finance, engineering, and operations; a new product-development project might be evaluated by a strategic planning group with representatives from marketing, engineering, and the executive office; an ERP (enterprise resource planning) system acquisition might be evaluated by representatives from virtually all divisions and most departments; and a new information-security system might be evaluated by representatives from IT (information technology), human resources, marketing, sales, and legal. The makeup of such coalitions is enterprise dependent, not always representative of all affected parties, and always contains inherent conflict among the participants.

The nature of conflict within coalitions stems from two basic sources, distinguished as organizational and individual. Organizational conflict comes from the internal competition for limited resources as well as the conflicting goals and strategies of different departments. For instance, engineering, R&D, and operations are typically in competition for a limited total capital expenditure budget. R&D, sales, HR, and legal are quite likely to have incompatible desires for an information-security system. The selection of a single-vendor ERP system may force compromises or power plays in all departments. And it is often typical that the goals of finance and purchasing departments are in conflict with the values sought by virtually all other departments. These conflicts are not necessarily unhealthy per se, but do exert a strong influence on decision making.

Though coalition participants are idealized as having the best interests of the organization in mind, they in fact give priority to personal interests related to both their employment and personal lives. For instance, a soon-to-retire manager may want a graceful exit with honors for past deeds as opposed to responsibility for something new and uncertain, a manager who is retiring in twelve months is already thinking about the transfer of responsibility and the things that will be said of competency when gone, and the manager with a pending promotion that could be jeopardized or delayed by a messy project in process will decide accordingly. A Decision Maker with responsibility for implementation, who has fallen behind the technology curve, may privately fear inadequacy and exposure. Inadequacy is not limited to an individual's self-evaluation, but includes the private perceptions held of the implementation team.

Everyone who evaluates a proposition gives priority to personal gain. Healthy people cannot be self-destructively altruistic, and do not hold an organization's goals above their own. People tend to work in organizations with compatible goals, for when this is not the case, a move to another organization occurs eventually, one way or another. The end result is that individual Decision Makers will generally satisfy both their own needs and those of the organization, but when there is a conflict, personal needs will be satisfied first.

Conflict notwithstanding, a coalition does arrive at a decision, and can therefore be looked upon as a Decision Maker in its own right, with behavioral characteristics at least as relevant as those of each participating Decision Maker. Much more will be said of this later.

A Champion can be conflicted as well. Champions can be characterized as skilled, unskilled, or conflicted in their construction and presentation of the value proposition. In all three cases they act as the advocate and principle speaker for the proposition; but in the conflicted case they have an indirect relationship to the proposition. The relationship is indirect in that the conflicted Champion is either drafted into the role as an otherwise uncommitted third party, or comes to the role as some sort of partner by virtue of a related but separate proposition. For instance, it is not uncommon for a complete enterprise-technology solution to require multiple suppliers, or for a supplier with weak credentials or an incomplete solution to seek partnership with one complimentary but stronger, or for a departmental manager wanting a particular IT problem solution to seek the expertise of an IT resource as Champion. Cases where a Champion is drafted include the use of consultants or internal resources chosen to champion the cause when a natural sponsor is preoccupied with other tasks or feels insufficiently skilled.

The conflict with partnerships is typically one of priority. It can manifest itself as inadequate knowledge of what is to be championed, an incompatible view of the problem seen from the partner's solution perspective, or as an unresolved division of responsibility in supplying the total solution. Drafted Champions are conflicted by a combination of two factors: they neither suffer nor enjoy post-decision consequences, and their strategy is indirectly focused by the sponsor they represent rather than directly focused by the real-time interactive dynamics of value propositioning.

Conflict notwithstanding, such usually conflicted relationships can be effective under the right conditions. For example, one relatively new company with an innovative technical solution for electric utilities is finding advantage in working as a subcontractor to a well-known CAD supplier, who brings the necessary credentials and prime-contractor guarantees in return for additional workstation seats that will be needed. Conflict is minimal and the Champion relationship is not delegated, but rather done in parallel.

The remaining two cases of the skilled and unskilled Champion share a strong level of undivided commitment, but are distinguished by both the skill and experience the Champion brings to the process.

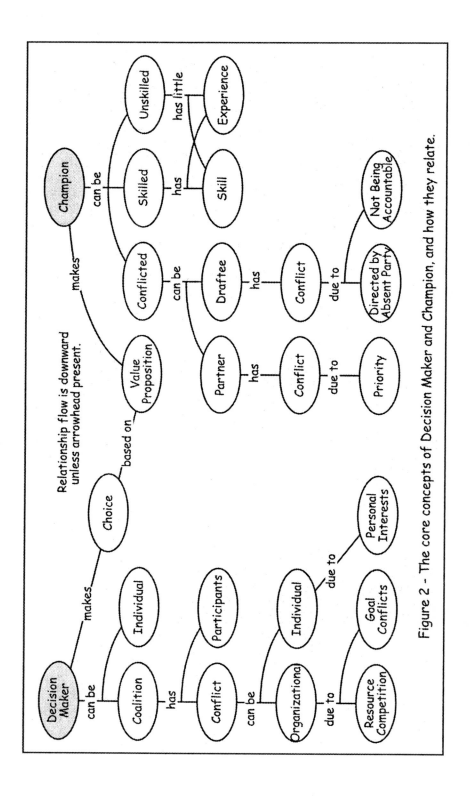

Figure 2 – The core concepts of Decision Maker and Champion, and how they relate.

The unskilled Champion's focus is dominated by the nature of the solution being proposed, typically confusing features for values. Decision Makers are credited with more understanding of the proposed solution than is likely, and are addressed as a unified rational group. A full understanding of the problem in its total enterprise context is not evident. The unskilled Champion does not recognize the process of value propositioning as a relevant skill, and proudly displays solution features of no relevance to the problem as perceived by Decision Makers. Passion and faith fuel the effort, which can be sufficient when Decision Makers are predisposed to the candidate solution, competing solutions are clearly inferior, or competing Champions are equally unskilled or conflicted. Common examples include the product-development project championed by a technically innovative engineer with no sense of the business environment, or the technically enamored entrepreneur bringing a new feature-rich product to market that can solve problems people don't give priority to as yet.

In contrast, the skilled Champion's focus is dominated by the nature of the problem and the nuances of individual Decision Maker perceptions. A broad base of knowledge relevant to the enterprise context is displayed. Solution features are tied to values, which are tied to relevant problem issues and objectives. Simplicity and tangible competitive differentiation are favored over complexity and unverifiable claims. The skilled Champion is a student of the process; recognizing the key role that mastery of value propositioning plays in personal success, whether that is in business management, technical management, or account management.

3

On the Nature of Problems and Solutions

As decision-making factors, problems and solutions are both personal perceptions of the mind, rather than facts or objects of truth. No two people affected by either will have absolutely identical perceptions. A problem perception is created by the dissatisfaction or pain that is felt or imagined by a Decision Maker confronted with a problem. A solution perception is created by a Champion's attempts to communicate a value proposition to a Decision Maker.

A Champion must understand how a problem is perceived by the Decision Maker in order to recognize relevant solution values. Each individual Decision Maker possesses a perception of the problem, which shapes and defines relevant values, and become requirements of an acceptable solution. The Champion must discover and understand this problem perception, and then select those aspects of the solution that address the values created by it. The perception of a solution is then created in the mind of a Decision Maker by the value proposition.

Perception is not related to truth, accuracy, or completeness. The perception a Decision Maker has of a problem is likely to be incomplete in the eyes of a Champion who has seen a variety of similar but different perceptions elsewhere.

Nothing happens until a problem is perceived by a Decision Maker. Then, and only then, do values come into existence that define an acceptable solution. The solution does not create values. The Champion does not create values. The Decision Maker's perception of the problem creates values. Ironically, however, a

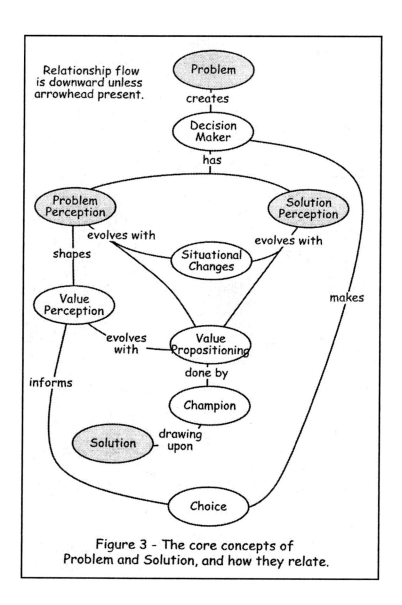

Figure 3 - The core concepts of
Problem and Solution, and how they relate.

Decision Maker may have to be introduced to the nature of a solution before a problem perception emerges, as is the case often with unsolicited proposals and innovative engineering ideas or business strategies.

Since problem perceptions are in people's minds and not writ in stone, they continuously evolve. Some of this evolution occurs as more knowledge is acquired, typically from exposure to new candidate solutions and new Champions attempting to differentiate their own solutions with unique features. And some of this evolution occurs when knowledge is refiltered and reprioritized as a Decision Maker's focus is changed by ongoing business and personal events.

Problem perceptions are dynamic in another sense as well. Skilled Decision Makers understand that the nature of the problem will continue to change over time as the situation and context surrounding it continues to change. For example, organizational growth through merger or market success will change the required capabilities of enterprise infrastructure technology, innovations by competitors will change the required capabilities of products and production processes, and the effects of economic cycles and market uncertainty change the requirements for flexibility.

Common traits among unskilled Champions include behaving as though solutions are unambiguous facts that speak for themselves, that solutions are perceived by Decision Makers as they are by Champions, that everything solutions are capable of delivering is relevant to a Decision Maker's perception of the problem, and that problems are perceived identically by all in a decision-making coalition. We will explore these behaviors later.

It is natural for Champions to feel ownership for the solution they represent, and to believe that the knowledge they have defines its nature. However, as skill develops, the Champion comes to understand that the Decision Maker's perception of their particular solution is the only definition that matters, and that responsibility for that perception lies with the Champion. The skilled champion also comes to know that the perception of the solution only exists in the context of the perceived problem. This awareness shifts the Champion's focus to the discovery and communication of knowledge, the nature of which we will take up next.

4

On the Nature of Knowledge and Context

A Decision Maker, like any human, acts only in accordance with knowledge. The knowledge that each of us has is a personal and idiosyncratic interpretation of the world around us. It is what drives every action we take and every reaction we have, large or small, moment to moment. It is what we know, and it is being continuously modified and updated as we are exposed to information and experiences throughout each day. All interactions between a Champion and a Decision Maker are part of this process, so there is great value for the Champion to understand this learning dance. It is, above all else, what will determine the action taken by the Decision Maker.

The skilled Champion recognizes knowledge and information as two different things, importantly distinguished by meaning. For example, demonstrating a particular technical feature present in a product without relating that feature to a valued benefit provides information without meaning. It floats in isolation, unconnected to what the Decision Maker knows. Similarly, a project Champion informed on the total development budget for the coming year, but uninformed on other projects competing for that budget, or having no concept of how they all relate to the organization's strategies and priorities, has information, but not meaningful knowledge.

Scholars of the mind, and how it absorbs new knowledge, tell us that information only becomes knowledge when its relationship to existing information or knowledge is explicit and interesting. Information unrelated, or too distantly related, to what is already known, is not absorbed. It is not linked to what matters, and therefore exerts no influence on action. Shortly after exposure it cannot even be recalled, except perhaps as a rote remembrance of utterance. We will explore more of this later, for the single most important skill a Champion wields is the creation of the Decision Maker's appreciation for value and its causes.

Like Decision Makers, Champions are also creatures delimited by their knowledge. While value propositioning, the Champion employs knowledge from two categories: possessed knowledge, which qualifies the Champion to undertake the process of value propositioning, and developed knowledge, which is learned and applied in real time by the Champion during the process. Necessary possessed knowledge includes the capabilities of the solution being proposed, the class of applicable problems addressed by the solution, the capabilities of potential competition, and the skills of value propositioning. Necessary developed knowledge includes the decision-making process, the Decision Maker's evolving perceptions, and the capabilities of the competing solutions.

Though few of us are highly skilled professional poker players, we all have some appreciation of what that involves. When rational, none of us would sit in a money game, no matter how small the stakes, without first knowing the hierarchy of winning hands, knowing the rules of the game being played, and having some perception of the methods and odds for improving a hand. If the stakes were high, we would also feel inadequate without some skill at learning our opponent's abilities and strategies during the game, and having some skill at influencing the opponent's perception of our hand.

A perception is formed in context. The Decision Maker's problem perception, for instance, is not generally as broad as what the Champion's solution is prepared to address. For example, the problem may be perceived narrowly in terms of the immediate corporate strategy, or specific departmental performance objectives, or a competitor's advantage, or new customer demands— and the budget and time constraints involved. Context establishes the Decision Maker's priorities and focus. It determines what is meaningful and interesting, independent of what is possible.

Value perceptions, problem perceptions, and solution perceptions are all formed in the specific context of the Decision Maker's environment. Consequently, understanding the Decision Maker's

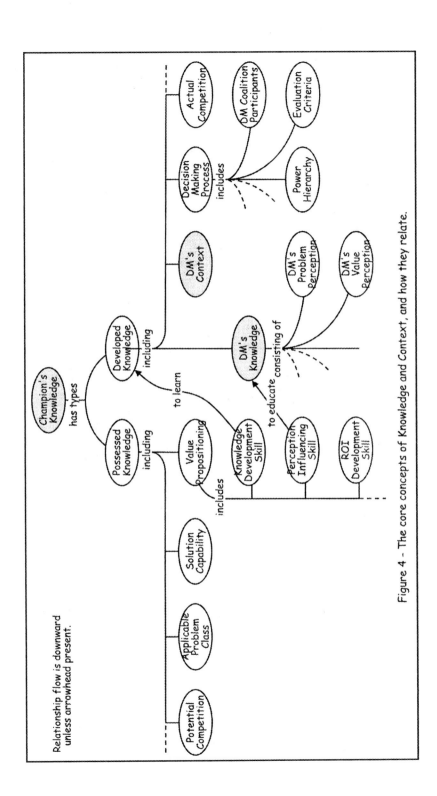

Figure 4 - The core concepts of Knowledge and Context, and how they relate.

context is often the most important knowledge for the Champion to learn.

The Japanese business style is well known for a protracted initial period of relationship development. Many meetings are devoted to understanding each other's general business goals and each other as individuals. A lot of time is spent in conversation and activity seemingly unrelated or quite distant from the specific nature of the intended business relationship. Westerners seeking business with Japanese firms during the late twentieth century were typically impatient and confused by this process, not realizing that the Japanese were building context-rich understandings that would help predict behavior of partners under unforeseeable and changing business conditions. Value-proposition development in Western settings doesn't usually have the luxury of slow and deep prerelationship development, so accelerated methods for ascertaining the context that shapes decisions must be employed.

We value people with relevant experience over those with youthful intellect because they understand context. The advantage that experience has over raw intellect is that it knows context deeply and personally from having been there and done that. The experienced person has built a rich working pattern of knowledge over time, and understands unspoken relationships and realities that affect the success of a solution to a problem. They enjoy respect and trust from the Decision Maker as a result—precisely because context is understood.

A good value proposition is both logical and functional, meaning it provides a consistent and complete model of features which address the requirements under consideration, and it facilitates an unambiguous assignment of benefit values. A superior value proposition, however, is a work of art: It has an inescapable quality about it that is easily recognized. It conveys a resonance with the organizational systems and culture that will affect its acceptance and fit, well beyond the stated requirements of the problem itself. It is compatible. It feels comfortable. It feels right.

In competition for approval, the Champion with the highest and most comprehensive understanding of context knows concepts and relationships that can produce values unseen by others.

5

On the Nature of
Trust and Risk

A value proposition is only a promise. At its best it is a consistent and comprehensive plan complete with an implementation roadmap. But it provides no real value until after it is implemented and delivering on the promise.

Every Decision Maker harbors some doubt about the certainty that any value proposition, no matter how well crafted, will be translated during implementation into a conforming delivery of its promise. The Decision Maker perceives this uncertainty as risk, and this perception of risk is part of the Decision Maker's perception of a solution's total composite Value. In many technology projects, especially information technology projects, failure to deliver even an acceptable approximation of the promise has become too common and has greatly increased the perceptions of risk for such projects.

Risk is inherent in all value propositions and value perceptions, whether explicitly itemized and addressed or not. Typically it is an invisible, unspoken factor, highly subjective in the mind of each individual Decision Maker yet extremely influential in the weighted hierarchy of values that result in a decision. Three principal areas of risk can exert influence on the Decision Maker: execution performance, user acceptance, and decision correctness.

Execution-performance risk is associated with the implementation delivering a result as specified, as budgeted, and as scheduled. This is the principal area where dissatisfaction with past results has raised the general level of uncertainty.

The risk of user acceptance is another rising trend associated with historical results, though not as widely respected as yet, as the consequences are neither as evident nor as easily accountable to a responsible party.

Finally, the risk of decision correctness is basically a self-doubt concern on the part of a Decision Maker, who is uncertain as to whether enough is known about the true nature and importance of the problem, uncertain about the sufficiency of the pool of candidate solutions being considered, and uncertain about what will be discovered when a new solution has unintended consequences or reveals knowledge that should have been factored into the decision-making process.

The perception of risk is typically very influential and personally subjective. Failed technology projects are often career damaging, or at least career momentum stalling, whether it is a new product that does not get to market on time, an ERP system that costs three times as much and takes three times as long as expected, or an expensive information-security system that creates more problems than it solves.

"They will trust me and my team to make it work" is the unskilled Champion's expectation. Trust is a major perception in reducing the perception of risk. But the perception of trust does not come as a matter of course. It comes because it is earned, because it is maintained, and because it is respected by the Champion as the principal tool for mitigating the perception of risk.

A useful model of trust characterizes it as a perception that develops in three sequential stages The first stage is based on control, where a new and untested relationship is trusted to work properly because there are enforceable means of providing rewards and penalties consistent with performance. The second stage of trust is based on predictability and develops when there is enough knowledge present to believe that behavior can be predicted. Trust at this stage does not necessarily expect good or bad behavior; it simply expects behavior to be predictable. The third stage is based on shared values and develops when past working experiences consistently strengthen a belief that shared values exist and will drive behavior in the best interest of the trusting party.

The key concept of this trust model is that the depth and breadth of knowledge that the Decision Maker has of the trustees is what determines the degree of trust possible. Thus, the more a

Decision Maker knows of a solution and its fit to the problem, the less uncertainty. The more a Decision Maker knows of the Champion's effectiveness and dedication as an ombudsman in the postdecision activity, the less risk will be perceived. The more a Decision Maker knows of the execution plan and the execution team, the less risk will be felt. The extreme of uncertainty occurs with the totally unknown, and is dismissed easily by the Decision Maker's fallback: "Better to deal with the devil you know than the devil you don't."

Trust is a belief that implementation will be executed properly. Some of this comes from the reputation of the execution team or the company providing a solution, and some from the reputation of the Champion. The old saw "Nobody ever got fired for buying from IBM" may no longer be true, but it reigned for decades as a prime example of minimizing personal risk and carried a formidable value for competitors to overcome.

Trust in the Champion is a belief that the Champion has the Decision Maker's best interests in mind. Trust in the solution is a belief that the solution both addresses the real problem, regardless of differing perceptions, and does so in a way acceptable to the users of the solution. Thus, trust in the solution can mitigate uncertainty of both decision correctness and user acceptance.

Sufficient knowledge to generate trust can, in some cases, indicate a solution is incorrect. This knowledge also removes uncertainty and lowers risk as a result, and will generally increase trust in the Champion who positively aids in that realization. The Champion who is in it for the long run will have a more valuable reputation as a result and come back another time enjoying an increased degree of trust.

Note that both uncertainty and trust, in the context here, are subjective, idiosyncratic perceptions, not facts of nature, or even facts of probabilistic certainty. Trust is hope and faith rooted in knowledge. Uncertainty is fear and skepticism rooted in the lack of knowledge. They are two sides of the risk coin and major factors in Value assignment.

Risk exerts its strong influence on total Value assignment for two reasons. Firstly, a general propensity for risk aversion is an observable and known behavioral phenomena in decision making, meaning risks are weighted more heavily than comparable rewards. Much more will be said of such human behavioral realities when we

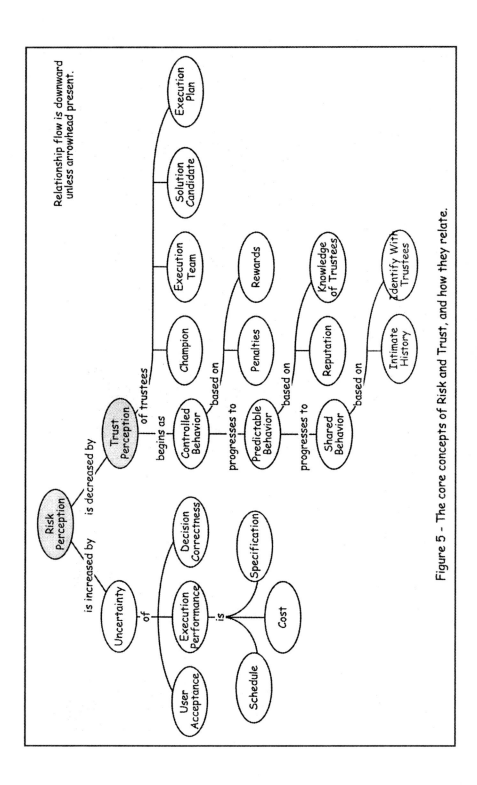

Relationship flow is downward unless arrowhead present.

Figure 5 – The core concepts of Risk and Trust, and how they relate.

look at Nobel Prize–winning research characterizing how people really make decisions as opposed to how we wish or think they should. Secondly, technology and technology projects have failed dramatically and with alarming frequency to deliver on plan, creating a general reception of skepticism.

6

On the Nature and Effect of Competition

Competition for approval, even if only against the status quo, is what creates Champions. Without competition there is no functional purpose for a Champion. The Champion is needed precisely because effort and argument is required to gain approval from Decision Makers. A sales account manager invited to verify assumptions held by Decision Makers who are ready to place an order does not engage in the act of Championing. A technical manager permitted to run with a proposed program without argument under threat of disapproval does not engage in championing activity. This point is made to crystallize the notions that competition is always present when a Champion is required to advance a value proposition and that the Champion's objective is to win approval.

With this understanding we see that to win approval the Champion must accomplish two things: help the Decision Maker perceive the proposed solution as at least adequate, and score a higher Value than all other competitors. Thus, we see that it is actually the other competitors who establish the minimal winning Value score, and, by the same reasoning, it is the other competitors who establish the nature of the game, for they will attempt to help the Decision Maker perceive the problem in terms that fit their particular benefits advantageously. This is what Champions do.

From this we see that the important competition is not so much between solutions, as might be expected, but rather between Champions, who are pitting their skills at value propositioning. The relative values of competing solutions are perceptions built by

27

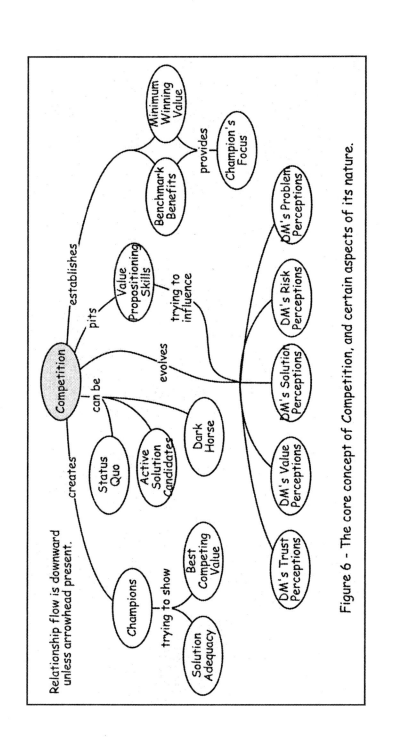

Figure 6 - The core concept of Competition, and certain aspects of its nature.

Champions in the minds of Decision Makers. This act of championing in competition is similar to the act carried out by advocates in a court of law, each arguing an opposing view, each attempting to establish different values in the minds of a judge or jury, and each knowing that the winner is more often determined by the most capable advocate rather than the most just cause.

Competition comes in three forms: active solution candidates, the status quo, and what can be called "dark horses." Active solution candidates are those actively participating in the competition to solve a problem. The status quo is the existing situation, which in the minds of Decision Makers could be sustained if a solution candidate doesn't provide compelling Value. On occasion the status quo is an active solution candidate in its own right, complete with a Champion who will argue its case. Even when the status quo is not an active competitor, each Decision Maker has an internal voice championing that cause. Dark horses can be especially problematic, in that they are not active candidates during much of the competition, but surface at some late stage, often with high differentiation from the active solution candidates and sometimes with precast Decision Maker preference.

Competition creates a dynamic environment as Champions jockey for the top position, changing the Decision Maker's value perceptions and problem perceptions continuously. Until a choice is made and final, having the highest Value at any point only compels another Champion to try to change the game and the values. Changing the game means changing the problem perception. Establishing the end-game score means changing the value perception. This dynamic is present even when a Champion's interaction with Decision Makers is limited and restricted, such as when written responses to written requests are the only form of communication.

The skilled Champion values competition because it defines the task and provides focus.

7

On the Nature of Competency and Talent

As we have seen earlier, there is considerable difference between a skilled and an unskilled Champion. Where technically focused people are involved, this difference stems typically from a lack of awareness that accepting the responsibility of being a Champion means agreeing to a competition, and often also from a lack of desire to compete on a personal level, as well as an inherent disdain for the cheap and ignorant tactics misassociated with competitive selling. Such an unskilled Champion shirks professional responsibility behind an attitude of righteousness. Where sales-focused people are involved, the unskilled Champion is differentiated typically by a storehouse of superficial and incomplete knowledge, and often also by a competitive focus limited to price concessions and brand reputation, as well as a disdain for recognizing the problem at hand as unique with nuance and detail that must be learned. Such an unskilled Champion shirks professional responsibility behind a reliance on luck and a strongly in-demand brand. Unskilled Champions in both arenas are sufficiently ineffective against skilled Champions to warrant no further discussion here.

Skill is a concept generally associated with trade crafts involving physical work, where competency requires learning in both the mental and physical sense. When the apprentice has been exposed to all of the basics and demonstrated sufficient competence to produce an adequate level of consistent quality, graduation to journeyman status occurs. The new journeyman embarks upon a career-long journey of self-improvement, responsible for improving and polishing entry-level competency through practice and peer learning. Some who are especially committed to the path of improvement may eventually attain the status of master, bringing to bear a plane of understanding recognizably higher than accomplished journeymen. The arts have a similar path, when those such as chefs, musicians, and painters are lauded as talented when they exercise master-class understandings.

Though value propositioning appears to be mental, or knowledge work, without a physical component, there is a necessary part of value-propositioning skill that is related to engaged, real-time, "hands-on" feedback and response—"hands-on" in the sense that the skilled Champion attentively feels the way through each engagement, using the constantly evolving shape of Decision Maker perceptions as a real-time guide for strategy.

To be skilled at value propositioning requires five prime component skills: financial ROI development, risk-reduction trust building, real-time learning, Decision Maker education, and communication clarity. Lacking some appreciation and facility with any one of these component skills, the Champion falls short of being competent for the task.

The words *competent* and *competitor* stem from a common root, as the one is a state of readiness to engage in the other. To be competent is to be qualified, capable, and fit to engage in a practice. The competent Champion is qualified and capable by having some facility with all of the five prime skills, and consciously employs four modes of thought while engaged in practice: a focus on the fundamental concepts, a sensitivity to cause-and-effect logic, a tuning of strategy in accordance with decision-making behavior, and a constant improvement in the ability to respond competitively. More on each of these now.

The fundamental concepts of value propositioning have all been introduced at this point, including this current characterization of competency and talent. Collectively these concepts and their relationships encompass the core body of knowledge a Champion brings to bear in skilled value propositioning. That competency and talent are included among the fundamental concepts is recognition that awareness of skill, its constituent elements, its state of development, and its potential range actively shape the Champion's expectations, strategy, and respect for the competition.

Cause-and-effect logic recognizes that the ultimate effect sought by the Champion is the Decision Maker's approval. The logic that causes this effect is explored in the second part of this book. Decision Makers are people, not analytical engines. Observation shows that they reach conclusions and make decisions with imperfect knowledge, biased understandings, unresolved conflicts, distracted focus, yet general satisfaction. Too much popular advice and assumption is predicated on how things ought to be done, instead of how they are inevitably done. Consistently effective Champions have developed an intuitive feel for this behavioral logic, which, as will be shown later, is confirmed by an impressive and undeniable body of studied behavioral analysis.

Tuning strategy to the logic of behavioral decision making respects the way things are likely to be, as opposed to the way they ought to be, or even they way they are proclaimed to be. All Champions, skilled or not, do some of this unconsciously, because they do swim in the same human behavioral waters as Decision Makers, but the skilled Champion also consciously employs explicit knowledge of behavioral logic in developing a value-proposition strategy. Book Two will explore aspects of behavior-tuned strategy.

The competent Champion's fourth mode of thinking is a conscious continual improvement activity. A Champion in competition faces a dynamic situation that can change frequently and dramatically without warning. The ability to respond appropriately, effectively, and timely is what measures the maturing of competency. Competitive response improves unconsciously with experience as more knowledge naturally provides more options and more awareness. But the competent Champion recognizes that appropriate real-time response is at the core of successful competition and consciously develops explicit capabilities for dealing with uncertain and changing situations.

Skill also comes in the form of talent, a seemingly natural ability to easily excel at something competent people work diligently to achieve. People with talent seem to understand things in a much richer and deeper way. Their modes of thinking and their knowledge base appear to be different and more effective than those used in the practice of studied competency. Talent seems to draw upon a "second sight" in its creative activity. Mature, well-rounded talent easily outperforms the competent practitioner. In my experience, however, talent alone, when immature or unbalanced, is generally no match for studied competency.

A brief introduction to four thinking modes that manifest as talent is in order at this point. This will lay groundwork for later development in Book Two.

Contextual thinking, in the talented sense, is a natural holistic perception of an integrated hierarchy of cause and effect. A thing under consideration is not seen in isolation, but rather with the interactive context that governs its identity. A talented author invariably shows characters confronted by a demanding situation to be both driven and constrained in their response by the context of their life experiences and larger current situation. A Champion in this contextual thinking mode automatically sees a Decision Maker's solution perception constrained in terms of the Decision Maker's problem experience and perception.

Insightful thinking is pattern recognition that filters complex information into a meaningful essence, or fills in the blanks when information is incomplete. Insight typically comes from experience, where enough different variations of something have been experienced that an invariant but comprehensive pattern reveals itself. The Champion who has sought approval from the same Decision Maker multiple times may develop a sixth sense about the nature of that Decision Maker's evolving perceptions. The Champion who has addressed a solution to Decision Makers with similar backgrounds may understand a useful path of progressive education.

Empathetic thinking is the ability to imagine, to the point of experiencing, another person's reactions and perceptions to a situation. It has a foundation of both contextual and insightful thinking for sure, but goes further, providing a sense of what it is like to be that person in that situation. A Champion in this mode has a deep sense of how the Decision Maker's value perceptions relate to problem and solution perceptions.

The fourth mode I call "responsive," and it is one that automatically initiates or modifies action in accordance with new knowledge as it becomes known. The connection between knowledge and appropriate action is immediate and involuntary. Thus, there is a seamless response as knowledge is revealed by insightful, empathetic, or contextual thinking. Talented jazz musicians exhibit this mode when they jam, each working compatibly with what the others in the group are doing, as if they had rehearsed to perfection what is actu-

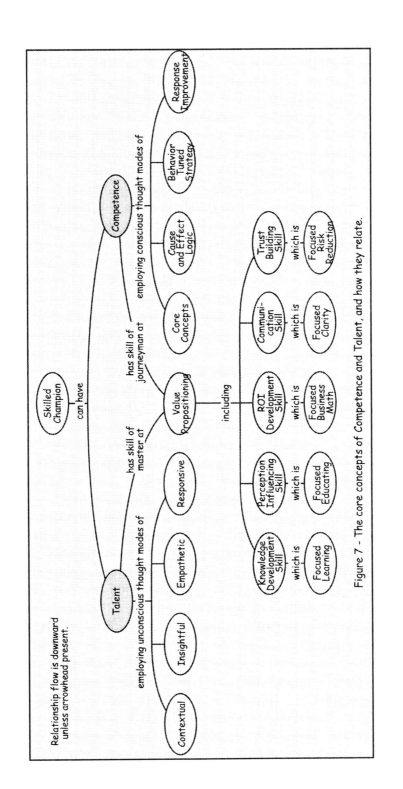

Relationship flow is downward unless arrowhead present.

Figure 7 - The core concepts of Competence and Talent, and how they relate.

ally an impromptu original performance. A Champion in this mode of thought expands a Decision Maker's solution perception in lock-step with the Decision Maker's evolving problem perception.

There is a lesson in this contrast of talent with competency. Michelangelo, when asked how he managed to sculpt such beautiful art, passed his talent off as merely removing superfluous material that was hiding what he clearly saw within the slab of marble. He, like many with creative talent, seem to have the effect they desire dominantly in mind, and use that clear vision to pull the mechanics of cause. Competent craftsmen, in contrast, seem focused on the mechanics of cause, pushing forward to achieve an effect. This contrast is not made to downplay competency, but rather to show the effects of focus and suggest that the Champion who would have superior skills must place driving focus on the problem and value perceptions of the Decision Maker, rather than on the nature of the solution or its perception.

The Champion who does not appreciate and nurture the craft and art of value propositioning relies on good luck and inferior competition to win approval. One may be competent or even talented as an engineer, but incompetent as a project Champion. Such a one may produce highly innovative design concepts, but be unable to convey their value to people making business decisions. One may be competent as a business manager, but incompetent at convincing executive committees to approve a proposed budget or strategy. Such a one may be an excellent manager of people and budgets, but ineffective when trying to communicate the value of an approach. One may be competent as a sales engineer, but incompetent in competitive sales situations. Such a one can help a prospect configure an appropriate and complex system and close a sale when the prospect has already chosen their brand, but fail consistently when a contest of Champions determines who closes the deal.

Part 2

Logic That Structures Core Concepts and Drives Decision Making

8

The Logic of Core Concepts

In the process of value propositioning there are two roles: that of the Decision Maker and that of the Decision Champion. Value propositioning is done in competition, so there are always multiple Champions, even when the only competitors to a sole active Champion are the inner voices of Decision Makers supporting the status quo. Decision making, though sometimes dominated or conducted by a single Decision Maker, is more often done by a coalition of Decision Makers when enterprise impact is involved.

Shortly we will look separately at logic that governs the behavior of decision making for both individual and coalition Decision Makers. To set the stage for those discussions, we look at the logic that determines the assignment of Value, regardless of the nature and behavior of the Decision Maker.

Value, with a capital V, you will recall, is a composite of many individual benefit values perceived by a Decision Maker. Value is reduced to a single measurement in order to allow comparison among competing alternatives. The Champion's objective is to cause Decision Makers to construct a Value from their perceptions that will win the competition, and therefore the Champion's goal is to influence these perceptions. This influencing activity is called value propositioning.

The process of value propositioning cannot begin until a problem is perceived, and cannot end until a superior Value directs a choice. Both the problem perception and the superior Value need some threshold of significance to initiate and terminate the process.

Though a problem is perceived, if it is not deemed significant enough by Decision Makers, value propositioning will not be entertained. Though a Value for a solution is perceived, if it is not deemed significant enough by Decision Makers, no action will be taken. Thus, we see that the value propositioning process is enabled by Decision Makers, and cannot occur without that enablement. All Champions in competition are not necessarily engaged in the process simultaneously, providing opportunity for those engaged earlier to develop more knowledge and exert more influence, should they have the skills to take advantage of this.

The Champion has only one channel for influence, and that is the value proposition. The Champion constructs the value proposition using skills of competency and talent applied to knowledge. This knowledge is the Champion's personal interpretation of information about the problem, the Decision Maker's context, the competition, and the solution being championed; and, most importantly, personal imagination of how information and competitive value propositioning is affecting the evolution of Decision Maker perceptions.

The Decision Maker's initial perceptions are personal interpretations of the problem and the decision-making context. The process of value propositioning then adds perceptions of values, risk, and trust associated with perceptions of solution candidates, and augments the initial perception of the problem. All of this occurs as the Decision Maker interprets the value propositions offered by each of the competitors.

From this it is clear that a Champion's value proposition does not speak for itself, any more than the Champion's solution speaks for itself. The Champion's solution, as perceived by the Decision Maker, is an interpretation of an interpretation, both constrained and filtered sequentially by the knowledge and ability of the interpreter. A value proposition does not speak for itself either, because the perceptions it hopes to cause evolve continuously as competitive value propositions cause new interpretations.

Effective competitors do not limit the focus of their value proposition to aspects of their solution alone, nor do they limit their competition-directed influencing to the problem perception, but in fact attack all perceptions that a Decision Maker may hold about a competitor's value proposition as well.

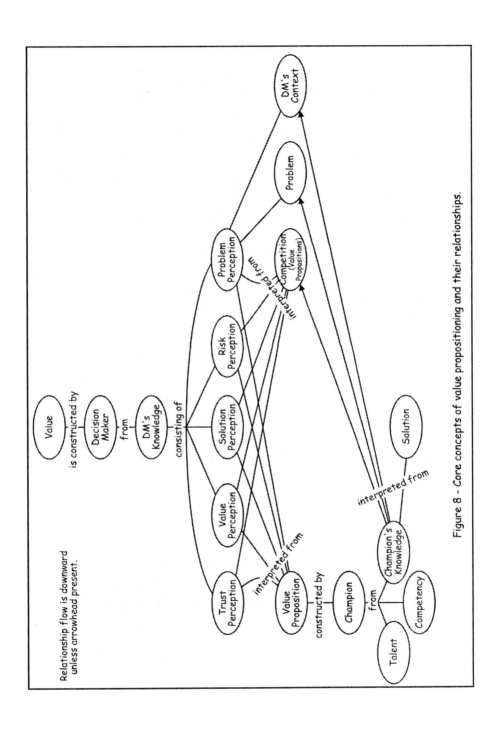

Figure 8 - Core concepts of value propositioning and their relationships.

Value propositioning is not a discrete event, but rather a dynamic process that is anticipated and managed by the effective Champion.

9

The Logic of Misperception

Gaining a favorable decision requires an interaction with Decision Makers that results in them having a favorable set of perceptions. This is a direct result of the Decision Makers' interpretation of the value proposition. The value proposition is a communication. As a communication, it is subject to miscommunication, possibly due to poor communication on the Champion's part, and definitely due to inherent human nature that filters and biases the perceptions obtained from the communication.

Research into the psychology of decision making has much to say about the mechanisms that inhibit perfect communication. None of this research conflicts with common sense or reflective observation on what we have all witnessed in practice, but it is comforting to know that there is rhyme and reason to what we might otherwise think is anomalous or serendipitous behavior.

I draw upon the overview developed by Scott Plous in his acclaimed book, *The Psychology of Judgment and Decision Making*, to organize this discussion of the mechanisms of misperception. The intent is to understand what is at work, so that later in Book Two we can discuss how strategy might be crafted to counter or reduce these effects, or even to leverage these effects to good advantage.

"Garbage in, garbage out" is a phrase embarrassingly applicable to how we all manage our memory and develop new perceptions. It comes with the wiring. There are both physiological and psychological reasons for this. The physiological reasons can be associated with differing roles of what is commonly attributed to the functions of the left and right brain, but won't enlighten this discussion sufficiently to concern us here. We will concentrate instead on the psychological mechanisms.

Misperception occurs principally during the acquisition of new knowledge, as opposed to later with study and refinement of existing knowledge. Recreating from memory what was witnessed at an auto accident is not unlike trying to remember what was shown in a demonstration of new technology, what was shown in a project presentation, or even what was read once in a written proposal. All of these events provide information that is selectively filtered and interpreted by the observer in the process of becoming memory and perception. Later, when recall is required, additional distortion occurs. The end result is a set of perceptions that are both incomplete and different than the original information.

We will discuss four kinds of distortion that occur during exposure to new information, and one that occurs during later recall.

Selective perception is a mechanism that interprets new information according to expectations and hopes. A Decision Maker generally has some hopes and expectations related to the problem at hand before considering any solutions. Learning research tells us that new knowledge can't be assimilated unless it relates closely to existing knowledge. Consequently, the existing knowledge of hopes and expectations exerts a subtle but strong influence on the interpretation of information. Something that is shown or told about a solution that does not relate to either may go unrecognized as something of interest. Shown or told things that do relate, but that are not consistent with these hopes and expectations, often causes a distorted perception of conformance. This means that there is a tendency to perceive what was presented as conforming to those hopes and expectations even if they do not.

Context dependence is a mechanism that interprets new information in terms of the context in which it was received, and comes in four varieties. Two of these, the *primacy effect* and the *recency effect*, are encountered when a Champion is given the option of being first to present or last to present in a series of competing presentations. The first presentation gains some dominance in the Decision Maker's perceptions sometimes, and the last presentation at other times. Research shows that this difference is related to the time that elapses between presentations and the decision event. If a series of presentations is relatively uninterrupted and then some time elapses before a decision is made, the first presentation has a dominance advantage. On the other hand, the last presentation gains a dominance advantage if time elapses between presentations but the decision is made immediately following the last. The *contrast effect* occurs when something is presented in the presence of something similar. Much like an average height movie star cast with shorter people gives the impression of the star as tall, so does a head-to-head competitive technology demonstration leave strong perceptions of any obvious differences. Finally, the *halo effect* occurs when one clearly dominant attribute of something develops a perception strong enough to influence the perceptions of other attributes. This can manifest in many forms, but a simple example is seen when Decision Maker's overrate specific benefits of a solution because of its leadership brand image.

Cognitive dissonance refers to a mechanism that seeks consistency, and can be responsible for changing old perceptions as well as creating new ones. If a perception already exists about something and new information wants to create a contradictory perception, one or the other will be changed in the receiver's mind to restore consistency. All fine and well if a falseness is being corrected; but this effect exists in important gray areas, such as when a Decision Maker's preconceived notion of something is confronted with a contradictory claim by a Champion. In this case either disbelief or enlightenment will be the result, often silently, and often whimsically. New perceptions can be created by this effect as well. Research shows that people often develop a perception of something in conformance with their unreasoned but spontaneous behavior or voiced opinion. That's what I think, and I'm sticking to it!

Hindsight bias is an interesting effect, and is associated with the predictability of uncertain cause-and-effect situations. It manifests as the creation of a perception, after the fact, that some specific outcome was expected and obvious all along, even though the person forming that perception would never have held that perception beforehand. It occurs, for instance, when one person relates to another the disaster that came of someone else's decision, and is met with an "Of course, that's obvious! I could have predicted that!" At least one person just formed a perception about the danger of duplicating that decision.

Memory bias is the last cause of misperception we will discuss here. Unlike the others, this is not about interpreting new information and turning it into biased perceptions, but rather about recall-

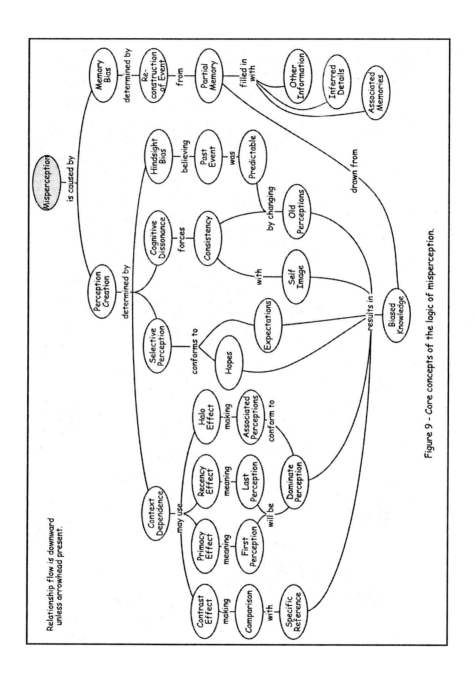

Relationship flow is downward unless arrowhead present.

Figure 9 - Core concepts of the logic of misperception.

ing knowledge necessary for an action such as a decision or a comparative evaluation. Research tells us that we appear to store memories of new information as related fuzzy concepts without all of the original detail. However, upon recall, the mind reconstructs a detailed remembrance. These details are supplied, unconsciously, by logical inferences about what must have been there as well, by association with similar memories, and by implications from other relevant information. This explains why five witnesses to the same auto accident remember contradictory and completely untrue event sequences. It also explains why Decision Makers sometime attribute one Champion's argument and benefits to another champion's solution.

The competent Champion is aware that communicating a value proposition effectively is tricky business. Competing Champions have the same handicap, so these effects should not confer advantage on any one Champion over the competitive long haul. Unless, of course, a Champion respects and understands these effects well enough to mitigate and leverage them. A discussion for Book Two.

10

The Logic of
Individual Decision Making

Soon we will explore the behavior of coalitions as Decision Makers. Now we look at the behavior of individuals as Decision Makers. These are not independent perspectives, however, as individuals in coalitions bring their decision making behavior with them.

How individuals make choices when offered alternatives has been shown to differ considerably from objective, optimal reasoning. Theories attempting to model what really happens abound, but one stands above all others in acceptance, principally for its coherence and its ability to predict actual behavior. *Prospect Theory*, as it is known, was developed by Daniel Kahneman, who shared the 2002 Nobel Prize in economics, according to The Nobel Foundation, "for having integrated insights from psychological research into economic science, especially concerning human judgment and decision-making under uncertainty." Nothing in this theory is surprising or in conflict with observations we are all familiar with. Its value here is that it details the psychological factors at work and itemizes the resultant biases in judgment. This discussion of individual decision making is my selective interpretation of Kahneman's work, principally based on the research he and Amos Tversky report on in their impressive collection of papers published as *Choices, Values, and Frames.*

Value propositions generally attempt to show multiple benefits, each stemming from some feature inherent in the solution and each promising to deliver some desirable value. Decision Makers, especially experienced ones, perceive value propositions as legitimate attempts on the part of a Champion to persuade, and so they hear each promised benefit with a bit of healthy skepticism—notably, in the information technology arena, with a good deal of skepticism. Subjectively they associate with each claimed benefit some uncertainty, or probability, of the likelihood that it will deliver as promised. Not because they disbelieve the Champion, but rather because they know from experience that honest claims assume ideal conditions of implementation, transfer, and acceptance. Such conditions are rarely itemized, and are unlikely to exist in any event: Implementations go bad, users reject, vendors get in trouble, schedules are underestimated, costs are underestimated, expected resources aren't committed, key personnel become unavailable, other priorities disrupt plans midway, and so forth. This historical record results in a Decision Maker assessing each claim with some subjective probability of likelihood.

The discussion will now explore ten behavioral results that stem from five psychological mechanisms which influence how Decision Makers arrive at valuation. Four of these behavioral results are associated with the weighting of probabilities, where the Decision Maker deviates plus or minus from some neutral assumption of the probability that a claim will be realized.

Valuation is knowledge dependant. A Decision Maker knowledgeable in the area of a benefit claim is likely to overweight the probability that it can deliver as promised, assuming that the knowledge is in agreement with the claim. Conversely, when little or no knowledge is present, the claim is likely to be underweighted. This is one example of why it is necessary to explain the connection between solution features and the benefits that they deliver, and to do so sufficiently that no ambiguity or vagueness remains in the mind of the Decision Maker. This exercises the education and communication skills discussed in Book Two.

Valuation is simplified. Various kinds of simplification are actively employed to reduce the complexity of evaluation and decision making. One standard procedure is to eliminate any claims deemed insignificant from further consideration. On the surface this may seem the best thing to do under all circumstances, but it has the effect of eliminating some claims and their values, small as they may be, that could swing the choice between two close alternatives when compared later. A claim may be deemed insignificant because its ability to deliver is considered highly unlikely, perhaps because it appears culturally or politically incompatible. A claim may also be considered insignificant because it simply is not appreciated as something to be desired, often for good reason, but sometimes due to an insufficient understanding. Another typical simplification is the chunking of probabilities. A subjective assumption of the probability that a claim will deliver is unlikely to be fine-grained. It is more likely that round numbers like 90% or 75% or 50% would be the assumption than 87.2%, for instance. Coupled with underweighting or overweighting, this chunking effect can result in some significant valuation swings.

Valuation is relative. The status quo typically establishes the neutral point for measuring value. Thus, a cost-reduction benefit is generally valued for the amount saved, independent of the total amount of cost, unless the amount is dismissed as insignificant. Likewise, new capability, increased productivity, faster response, better quality, and other such benefits are measured relative to a reference point.

The reference point is not, however, always the status quo, nor always a fixed point throughout a decision-making process. Sometimes the reference point is based on expectations, hopes, or what is believed possible. A Decision Maker seeking a specific performance objective will not value something that gets halfway there, even though it is twice as good as the status quo provides. Decision Makers seeking a reduction in some undesired quality, such as security risk, will recognize relative value for any solution that accomplishes that, until they learn it is possible to eliminate the risk completely. A product manger seeking a more competitive product will value project proposals relative to current competition rather than the current product, but change that reference point when shown an unexpected announcement by a competitor, or when shown a proposal for something different with the potential to obsolete the entire product concept.

The effective Champion knows the reference point as well as the potential for moving the reference point or finding it moved during the process. Relative valuation takes a different turn, however, when the problem has unacceptable consequences associated with it, such as business survival. The point of reference then is an unequivocal objective, and getting close is of no value.

Typically a candidate solution is measured against multiple objectives, and the valuation for each is rolled up into a representative total Value. Frequently a solution cannot offer positive gains on all objectives. One solution may offer gains in ease of use and speed of response, but with a loss of a familiar but marginally necessary capability present in the status quo. Another may offer twice the performance of the reference point but cost twice as much as well. These valuation measurements are all viewed as gains and losses relative to the reference point.

That valuation is perceived in terms of gains and losses is an important distinction. The perception of something as a gain instead of a loss, relative to a reference point, has strong psychological impact on valuation. Among other impacts, it affects the willingness to take risk.

Decision Makers are not, strictly by nature, either risk averse or risk seeking, as is often believed, but change behavior depending upon the options that face them. For example: A company that has decided to choose an integrated ERP system to replace a collection of poorly integrated independent applications is likely to find that it must give up some previously valued functionality. Quite possibly, all candidate solutions will be unable to meet some specific capability satisfactorily. Under these circumstances Decision Makers are more likely to consider otherwise marginal solutions that will provide the desired capability, even though there may be some higher risk associated with such a choice. This is the case where a high probability of loss creates a tendency for risk-seeking behavior. Risk-seeking behavior also surfaces when the situation shows low probability of gains, as when all solution candidates for an ERP system agree to develop custom code for a missing desired feature, but all have a track record for failing to deliver custom code on time. Risky solutions are also more acceptable when a problem has terminal implications, such as operating costs that will guarantee bankruptcy or product costs that spell market loss.

Conversely, risk-averse behavior is exhibited when a low probability loss is perceived, such as when an engineering project cannot guarantee that it will meet some specific performance mark, but the likelihood of missing it is fairly low. Under these conditions Decision Makers are not going to take a risk on some otherwise wild alternative just because it looks solid on that one desire. Risk-averse behavior is also seen with high probability gains, as in, "Why take a risk if it looks pretty sure that desires will be met by going down the safer path?"

Valuation is formulation dependant. Describing the same claim in different words and concepts can change the perception of loss or gain. It is known that most people are risk seeking, even when faced with the possibility of large losses. Yet the insurance industry thrives under situations like this, predicated on people's preference for suffering a sure loss (the cost of the premium) over the uncertain possibility of a larger loss. Decision research shows that couching loss-mitigating expenses as insurance can turn a loss perception into a gain perception. That there are differing perceptions of loss and gain is evident when a value proposition features the elimination of jobs, which may be viewed by some Decision Makers as a gain and by others as a loss. A manufacturing representative on the capital expenditures committee may view an engineering proposal as a loss of available capital for manufacturing, but this perception might be changed if a presentation showed the gain that manufacturing will realize due to the engineering investment.

Formulation effects are also evident in the order of presentation. Decision research shows that when concepts which establish a certain perspective are presented in series, one or a few that follow a strong one can ride the established psychological context. Subtle on the surface, perhaps, but when coupled with the misperception behaviors, we see a path for establishing unsubstantiated viewpoints. As Book Two will show, the Champion who pays attention to formulation effects can counter the formation of misperceptions discussed earlier.

Valuation is nonlinear. Initial increments of gain are valued higher than subsequent increments. People value the addition of $100 to a wallet with $100 already in it more so than the addition of $100 to a wallet already containing $1000. We value a 100% gain more than we value a 10% gain, even though the increment is identical, and generally we will pay more for the one than the other. Losses reflect the same diminishing return shape. Loosing $100 from a $1000 wallet is not felt nearly as badly as loosing $100 from a $200 wallet. This diminishing of value results in undervaluing incremental increases of gain. Reducing an uncertainty or risk from 10% to zero is a lot more valuable than reducing it from 25% to 15%. People value the elimination of uncertainty over simply reducing it, even when the amounts are equal. This is called the certainty effect, which appears to have an even stronger push from underlying psy-

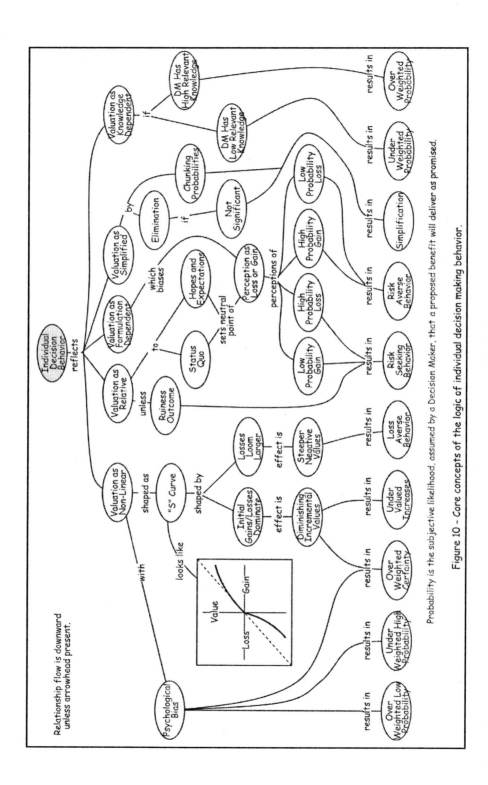

Figure 10 – Core concepts of the logic of individual decision making behavior.

Probability is the subjective likelihood, assumed by a Decision Maker, that a proposed benefit will deliver as promised.

chology than just from the diminishing returns of the loss-value function.

Diminishing losses are not symmetric with diminishing gains. "Losses loom larger than gains," the decision researchers affirm for us. One implication of this important distinction is that a gain and loss of equal value are not perceived as offsetting. Unless under mandate to reduce headcount, losing twelve people because technology can save their salaries is not typically considered an even deal by many real Decision Makers, in my observation. Another implication: Things we own appear to have higher value than we are willing to pay to reacquire them. This is called the endowment effect, and its classic example is the person unwilling to part with a special bottle of fine wine when offered $200 for it, but equally unwilling to buy the same bottle for $100. This faster decline of loss value, as compared to increase of gain value, accounts for the generally observed loss-averse behavior people exhibit.

Other psychological effects account for nonlinearity as well. Overweighting certainty was already discussed. It is also observed that people don't have good abilities to comprehend extreme probabilities, and as a result, behavior around very high and very low values is not certain. There is a tendency to overweight low probabilities, known as the "lottery effect" for obvious reasons. There is also a tendency to underweight high probabilities, however small the difference between certainty and high probability. It is also observed that people underweight high probability outcomes (perhaps skepticism) and overweight low probability outcomes (perhaps hopefulness: the lottery ticket example). "Because people are limited in their ability to comprehend and evaluate extreme probabilities, highly unlikely events are either ignored or overweighted, and the difference between high probability and certainty is either neglected or exaggerated," say Kahneman and Tversky.

11

The Logic of Group Decision Making

Herb Simon was awarded a Nobel Prize in Economic Sciences in 1978, according to The Nobel Foundation, "for his pioneering research into the decision-making process within economic organizations." In general, Simon is credited with founding the field of behavioral economics with his concepts of "bounded rationality," which broke from the classical notion that business decisions are made under optimal conditions and strive for optimal results. These concepts are described in his book *Administrative Behavior*, which the Nobel committee called "epoch-making," and form the basis for Kahneman and Tversky's work on individual decision-making behavior just discussed and for the "important work," according to Simon, of Richard Cyert and James March, published as *A Behavioral Theory of the Firm*.

Cyert and March offer that "the firm is, in fact, a coalition of participants with disparate demands, changing foci of attention, and limited ability to attend to all organizational problems simultaneously." They note that coalitions have inherent conflicts which remain unresolved, power politics and positions that often exert disproportionate influence, goals that might be ambiguously stated purposely to restrict knowledge of true intent, and other group-induced behavior that force departure from optimized, objective decision making. A coalition is of course a group of individuals, each of which brings to the party the misperception mechanisms and biased individual behaviors already discussed.

Three processes are of interest: objective setting, perception creation, and choice. In all three the nature of the problem perception plays an important foundation role, a common and oft repeated theme here. Before looking at these three processes, we will review six embedded concepts that deserve separate note: candidate-solution search, organizational slack, acceptable level rules, unresolved conflict, attention focus, and "satisficing."

Satisficing, in Simon's words, is the essence of what he calls bounded rationality: "Administrative theory is peculiarly the theory of intended and bounded rationality—the behavior of human beings who *satisfice* because they have not the wits to *maximize*." Under ideal conditions in an ideal world, Decision Makers are supposed to find and examine all possible solutions, maximizing the value obtained by selecting the best from among all those available. In reality, where time and attention are scarce resources, and complexity rules, the Decision Maker "looks for a course of action that is satisfactory, or 'good enough.' ... Because administrators satisfice rather than maximize, they can choose without first examining all possible alternatives and without ascertaining that these *are* in fact all the alternatives. Because they treat the world as rather empty and ignore the interrelatedness of all things (so stupefying to thought and action), they can make their decisions with relatively simple rules of thumb that do not make impossible demands upon their capacity for thought. Simplification may lead to error, but there is no realistic alternative in the face of the limits on human knowledge and reasoning." For the Champion this may be a two-edged sword. On the one hand it will tend to limit the field of competition. On the other, it will tend to oversimplify the problem and limit the benefits for consideration. Two edges can be wielded well, however, as will be seen in Book Two.

Attention focus is limited for Decision Makers. Generally all have other ongoing duties with daily deadlines and surprises which compete for attention. On top of this is the sheer complexity and impossibility of trying to anticipate all of the unintended consequences that will ensue from any decision. When limited available attention is directed at the decision-making process, it is focused where personal urgency is felt. This gives priority to a manageable subset of issues. Only so many things qualify for urgency at any one time, for any one person. Champions addressing issues outside of this perimeter don't gain value points for that effort, and risk losing or confusing the understanding of more relevant values.

Unresolved conflict is a natural artifact of modern organizations. The separation of responsibilities and objectives in a hierarchical structure pits different subgroups in competition for resources and strategic focus. Conflict is mitigated in coalitions through a variety of means, some natural and some imposed. Natural means are principally the result of limited attention focus. Some participants have immediate interests so sharp that longer-term conflicts are ignored or unseen. Imposed means have two forms of interest to us. First, objectives that may conflict across functions are prioritized in sequence. For instance, a production objective may require satisfaction before a marketing objective is given priority or even considered in the evaluation process. Second, the organization requires that decisions made by the coalition observe acceptable level rules, discussed next.

Acceptable level rules, Cyert and March tell us, circumvent conflicts that would otherwise deadlock a coalition or disenfranchise some participants. Basically they "require that local decisions satisfying local demands made by a series of independent decision centers result in a joint solution that satisfies all demands." They observe that one impact of this rule is the lowest common denominator effect. Satisfying *all* demands is possible, as they note that if no solution alternative can accomplish this, then either the coalition will find additional candidates to consider, or they will relax or eliminate demands to find a common acceptable level for all participants. The implication for a Champion is obvious: know the intersection of all individual demands, and either satisfy that condition or know at least that none of the competition can do this either.

Organizational slack refers to the operating efficiency, or leanness, of an organization at a specific point in time. When times are bad and downsizing has run its course, for instance, slack is at a minimum or nonexistent. Under these conditions decision mistakes that waste time or squander resources can be very costly, perhaps unrecoverable. Decision Makers are very wary and highly risk averse, and more inclined to search harder for strong solutions. In good times when cash is not a scarce resource, when general market growth is strong, or when competitive advantage enjoys strong market acceptance, organizational slack increases. Under these conditions risks with interesting reward potential can be viewed favorably, and satisficing is quicker to settle for acceptable solutions.

Search is the activity that identifies and selects candidate solutions for consideration. Satisficing behavior tends to limit search activity initially to a small number of candidates, and generally will not begin again unless the initial pool of candidates does not have an acceptable solution. Search is influenced by three factors: the current amount of organizational slack, who is in charge of the search, and, importantly, a tendency to look for candidates that are similar in nature to the existing unsatisfactory solution or to the perception of the problem. Thus, when an existing product becomes inadequate for the market, a company will tend to look purposely for projects that promise a superior featured version rather than something completely different that would obsolete the product concept. Similarly, if a company outgrows the capability of its current sales-management support system, it is more likely to look for one with more capacity rather than looking purposely for a different approach. An example of the problem perception directing the search is seen when a strategy that failed to address last year's goals instigates a search for a better strategy, rather than a reconsideration of the goals. There is an inclination to stay inside the box unless adequate solutions cannot be found. Unless, of course, the person in charge of the search process is an out-of-box thinker by nature, or for some other reason feels a more radical approach has compelling value. In any event, the person or subgroup in charge of the search has a dominant influence on which candidates will be considered. The final influence is organizational slack. When high, there are excess resources available to spend more time looking for more candidates. Satisficing will often counter this effect. Since high slack reduces the pressure to find an optimal fit, search may end when the first candidate is found that appears to meet all of the objectives.

The *objective-setting process* typically begins in advance of solution-search activity. It is not an isolated event in sequence, however, and evolves as perception creation evolves and as membership in the coalition changes. Objective setting, in the sense of what must be addressed by a solution, has two parts: identifying the nature of individual objectives and establishing the performance level for each. One semiconductor manufacturing company, for instance, that expected to grow through acquisition in a traditionally cyclic market wanted an "agile" IT strategy that had one objective aimed at the integration of acquisitions and another aimed at flexible costs. The performance targets for integrating a new acquisition were set at forty-five days for fully integrated financial reporting and at thirty days for fully integrating all acquired employees into the on-line HR systems, and performance for cost flexibility was not to exceed a certain percentage of revenue.

The list of objectives is principally influenced by two factors: the Decision Makers in the coalition and their individual objectives. In the semiconductor company example, the nature of the objectives would have been different if the coalition had not included representatives from corporate planning in addition to the participants from IT, HR, and finance. Individual coalition members also exert personal preference in setting objectives. If coalition membership changes before a final choice is made, it is quite possible that objectives can change as well.

The performance targets set for each goal are influenced principally by three things: past objectives, performance attained on those past objectives, and performance attained by other organizations on similar objectives. Citing the semiconductor company example again, targeting thirty days for HR system integration performance was based on published results of a leading company in a different industry. The roots of performance targets are sunk in the organizational learning that occurs from prior shared experience and observation, and is often unspoken context that the skilled Champion will seek.

The *perception creation process*, as seen previously, is an interpretation of value propositions. These value propositions are related to a specific pool of solution candidates generated from the search activity discussed above, and are influenced by five sources of bias worth noting: prior training and experience, unresolved conflict, attention focus, decision psychology, and simple patterns. We've discussed the nature and effects of attention focus and unresolved conflict above. Decision psychology was the subject of the discussions on misperception logic and individual behavior logic. That leaves simple patterns and training and experience remaining for discussion.

Simple patterns for developing valuation are the general rule, for two reasons. Firstly, accurate ROI comparisons are difficult to compute and subject to disagreement, so simply being affordable and clearly addressing the problem with improvement appear to be stronger influences. Secondly, though some argue that all things can be translated into costs, accomplishing this for all criteria is awkward and subject to disagreement, so settling on a small number (six, give or take) of mainly independent objectives is frequently observed.

Training and experience, of course, form the initial knowledge base that any Decision Maker starts with. Perceptions build upon this foundation only when new information is closely related to what is already known, facilitating incremental knowledge growth. Someone from finance participating in a decision for a CRM (customer relationship management) system, for instance, is likely to understand a sales-cost analysis much more readily than the features that improve personal interactions between customer and salesperson.

The choice process is the group's mechanism for selecting the final choice among alternatives. Typically this follows rules standardized by the organization. These standard rules determine how candidates are scored against objectives addressing the problem perception. They are based on the organization's past experience in scoring decision alternatives and consequently often reflect the organizational slack in the past when the rules were established. If they were established when slack was high, they are likely to be less risk sensitive than otherwise. If not, uncertainty may play a dominant role. In any event, organizational choice prefers to avoid uncertainty rather than carry it into the scoring process, when possible.

Uncertainty is avoided either by negotiating predictability with the winner or by recasting the objectives for a shorter-term solution that has sufficient predictability. If the decision choice involves an outside party, such as a product vendor, predictability is typically obtained with contract terms that guarantee results or extract a compensating penalty. If the decision involves inside projects, other funded projects may be required to compensate, if necessary. Where uncertainty is caused by an inability to see far enough into the future, objectives will likely be scaled back to fit within a shorter period of time.

Choice requires that the unresolved conflict inherent to decision-making groups be mitigated. As we saw earlier, this can also modify objectives, where compromise is made until all Decision Makers find acceptable common ground. Of course in any such

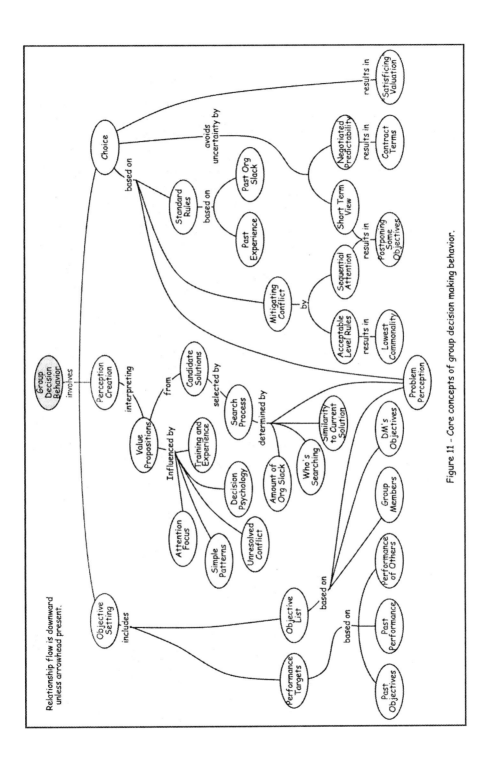

Relationship flow is downward unless arrowhead present.

Figure 11 - Core concepts of group decision making behavior.

group there are politics at work, and there are some Decision Makers with more say than others and some who dominantly influence others. The skilled Champion learns the relative roles of each Decision Maker, and knows that each must have satisfaction in the end.

Through it all, satisficing reigns. The group will search for an acceptable solution and be happy to make a decision once one is found. Faced with multiple acceptable solutions, the best among them will be desired, but not necessarily discovered. Instead, simplification will be employed to make the decision process manageable. In a strong satisficing situation, the order in which candidates are considered will have a major effect on outcome, for the first one that meets acceptable criteria is quite likely to trigger a decision and end the process.

12

The Logic of Perception Formation

Knowledge plays a central role in this discussion of value propositioning, so it is necessary to be precise about how that word is used.
Here, knowledge is that stuff we humans hold in our heads that
governs what we believe and how we act. This has nothing to do
with truth, accuracy, completeness or any other value judgment, nor
with science, philosophy, art, or any other body of revered theory
and practice produced by great minds. Knowledge is simply the stuff
we have in our heads that guides our behavior, as individuals. What
one person holds as knowledge has no bearing or necessary agreement with what another holds as knowledge, though it is likely that
there is a large enough overlap to keep both out of jail and away
from each other's throats. More than that may permit them to have
a useful discussion, maybe even an enjoyable association or working
relationship.

In this light, perceptions are knowledge, and knowledge is
formed by the process we call learning. So to understand perceptions meaningfully, enough to help cause favorable ones to form in
the minds of Decision Makers, we must have working models of
knowledge that can describe what it is and predict how it is learned.
For that we turn to David Ausubel and Josepf Novak. Ausubel published *The Psychology of Meaningful Verbal Learning* in 1963 and
Educational Psychology, A Cognitive View in 1968. Together these
books advanced a theory of learning that has had a large influence
on both practicing educators and learning-theory researchers ever
since. It is especially useful to us because it focuses on how people

learn from verbal and written presentations, the primary learning situation in value propositioning. Novak built on Ausubel's foundation a visual representation of knowledge he calls "concept maps," which appears to reflect the way we structure knowledge internally. Though the work of both men is simplified here, Ausubel's books referenced above, and Novak's books *Learning How to Learn* and *Learning, Creating, and Using Knowledge* can provide more depth for those who want a deeper understanding.

Rote learning is something most of us are familiar with from early schooling, when we memorized multiplication tables, dates of historical events, or poetry of no personal interest. Unless one is gifted with a photographic memory, this type of learning generally relies on dull repetition. In contrast, what Ausubel calls "meaningful learning" relies on associating some new piece of knowledge with something already known. The closer the association to what is already known, the more effective the learning. It is this association that provides meaningful linkage between new knowledge and prior knowledge.

Ausubel notes: "If I had to reduce all of educational psychology to just one principle, I would say this: The most important single factor influencing learning is what the learner already knows. Ascertain this and teach him accordingly." In addition to closely related prior knowledge, he also believes two other factors are necessary for meaningful learning: the learner must believe that learning the material will provide some value, and the learner must want to learn the material. These three conditions are not automatically present when a Champion addresses a Decision Maker. From my experience, one or all of these necessary conditions is missing far more often than not. If that means the Champion must rely on rote learning to have the many points of the value proposition remembered at valuation time, repetition repetition repetition would seem in order. Unfortunately this is not an option, as rote learning in this case is not a substitute for meaningful learning. Though the Decision Maker may well remember the irritating insistence of certain claims, if these claims are not tied into related prior personal knowledge, they float unsupported with no basis for belief.

In addition to the dimension that ranges from rote to meaningful learning, Ausubel also recognizes the dimension that ranges from discovery to presentation learning. Discovery learning occurs when someone engages in activity that results in reaching personal conclusions based on things they experience, like learning a new word processor by trial and error instead of reading the manual (on the rote end of the scale), exploring a free-trial offer for suitableness, or having an inspiration for a new market after playing with a prototype (the meaningful end of the scale). Presentation learning, on the other hand, occurs when a subject expert, such as the Champion, presents verbal or other prepared information to a learner, such as a Decision Maker. Most value propositioning is presentational in nature.

To explain the mechanisms of learning, Ausubel relies on a cognitive model of how knowledge is structured internally in our minds. It is suggested that our ability to know things arises from an ability to represent concepts in neural structures and to relate these concepts to each other in some meaningful association. For instance, at an early age we develop a concept of living things and another for nonliving things. At some point we develop a concept for pets, like the family dog and cat, which is different than the concept we have for people. But we associate both people and pets to the concept of living things rather than to the concept of nonliving things. The first association we develop between living things and people may be simply that they interact with us, whereas the nonliving play toy in the crib does not. This association and the two concepts it connects is meaningful because it can be acted upon. Either concept may exist without any association to another, but they are meaningless in isolation. As life progresses we develop large structures of concepts and associations that model the world as we know it. Assimilating new knowledge occurs when a new concept is associated with some concept we already possess, such as the concept of a crying noise associated with people as attention getting. New knowledge also develops when new associations are made between existing concepts, such as additional variations on attention getting, like hunger is alleviated by people when a crying noise is made. Hunger is likely one of the many initial hard-wired concepts that form the seed foundation for all subsequent associations to new concepts.

Novak has made this concept-association model of knowledge explicit, with an external visual representation he calls "concept maps," a term he has trademarked. His purpose was to provide a tool that can help people skillfully improve the learning process, either in others when they engage in teaching, or in themselves when they engage in learning. Both are pivotal skills for the effective Champion.

Every section of this book has included a concept map to visually summarize the central ideas. Partly this was done because it is known that many people are better as visual learners than as verbal or textual learners; partly because otherwise dense textual information becomes transparent in graphic form; partly because it is a succinct way to summarize the key points; partly because they were used to organize the thoughts for discussion; and partly, hopefully, because their usefulness has been self-discovered and appreciated.

Effective concept maps follow simple natural rules that reflect what seems to be the internal cognitive structure of *newly assimilated* knowledge: they must be hierarchical, in that concepts lower in the diagram are refinements of concepts higher in the diagram to which they are connected; relationships within a hierarchy are progressively refined and increased in number with subsequent learning; and with more learning, immature relationships are corrected, and cross-links from one hierarchy to another integrate more complex relationships. By convention, relationships are directed downward along connecting lines, as befits a hierarchy, unless an arrowhead is present to show differently. Also by convention, one should be able to read a meaningful thought when traversing connected concepts.

The *newly assimilated* distinction made above is important, for it appears that learning relies on a hierarchical structure of knowledge that is not necessarily maintained when initial knowledge matures to comprehensive expertise. For example, we have all had the confusing experience of listening to someone explain to us something they know very well, as they go round and round about things that make no sense. Politely listening long enough sometimes rewards us with dawning light. Things start to make sense. Things said earlier that made no sense all of a sudden have a logical relationship. But what an excruciating experience! Many things said earlier were immediately forgotten, and now must be repeated in the context of a structure that is all of a sudden apparent. Subject experts know the details and important nuances and low-level interactions so well that these have become the important and defining issues for them. They never really appreciated the gestalt of their subject until they could feel all of the pieces in simultaneous bal-

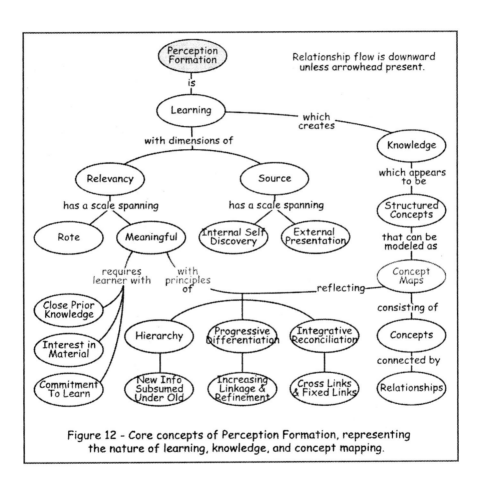

Figure 12 - Core concepts of Perception Formation, representing
the nature of learning, knowledge, and concept mapping.

ance. There is no longer a beginning and end for them, so they naturally dive right in to some arbitrary point and start describing their walk through the forest as a tree-by-tree experience, unaware of how they long ago built the scaffolding that allowed this understanding to emerge. The scaffolding is necessary to get started.

As learners it appears that we can easily assimilate things that are connected to other things we already know. Walking us from where we are to where we need to go a step at a time builds knowledge with meaning. A manned exploration program for Mars may have great and immediate benefit, but the program won't be valued by describing how the survival problems of keeping men on Mars will be solved. Describe first the logic of why going there meets known needs here and now on Earth, or if such needs are not well known, back up further until there is a familiar place to begin the education process ... and I will follow you anywhere, even to Mars.

Concept maps are explicit versions of natural tools we all employ, even when we don't make them into diagrams. It is how we learn, and it is how we teach when we are effective teachers. To repeat Ausubel again: "If I had to reduce all of educational psychology to just one principle, I would say this: The most important single factor influencing learning is what the learner already knows. Ascertain this and teach him accordingly."

13

The Logic of Multi-objective Valuation

Value propositions are rarely evaluated on a single objective. Generally a solution will be graded on a number of objectives. Some of these objectives will be considered more important than others. The prototypical approach involves establishing a list of key objectives, assigning relative weights of importance to each, scoring individual solutions against each objective, multiplying the individual objective scores by the weights, and totaling the result for each candidate. A comparison of the totals reveals the highest-scoring candidate, which presumably becomes the choice. A proposal for a new product, for instance, may be graded on objectives that include total cost, how fast it will return the cost with profits, the multiple of the original cost that profits are projected to earn in a specific period of time, and the market share it will secure. Each of these objectives generally has threshold requirements on them that define acceptable candidates. If investment cash is especially scarce, the original cost objective may be weighted higher than all of the others. If not, market share may have a higher weighting, if that is an important strategy requirement, or the profit multiple on cost may be viewed as more important than others. In any event, each of these also has some risk of actually occurring as estimated, which may be a factor that is also explicitly used as a multiplier along with importance weighting. Evaluating competing purchase candidates from vendors is no different, though likely to have more objectives, and also likely to have more objectives that are considered intangible, which can be difficult to score with confidence and consensus among a group of Decision Makers.

Decision theory offers many alternates to this simple linear model of multi-objective valuation, attempting to remove the human behavioral biases from decision making. Some of these are exceedingly complex in the number of objectives that should be considered, the proper ways to measure objective scores, and wide departures from this simple weighting and totaling structure. Detailed methodologies and software tools are available to handle these complexities to help ensure an objective optimal decision. When value propositioning is completed, a final choice is likely to be justified by its score in a formal and approved evaluation model. Typically, however, decision makers feel that they lose control of the decision-making process with these tools. Gut-level instinct rules.

Earlier it was suggested that Decision Makers form personal preferences well before any final and explicit analytical comparison is made among alternatives and that these personal preferences influence the process of analysis to produce a Decision Maker's desired outcome. Analytical decision methodologies are only as good as the input that drives them, and this is where subjective preference exerts its will. Gut-level preferences have a very influential effect on final choice, regardless of what analytical methodologies are formally employed to justify the result as being objective.

These preferences are present before formal value propositioning is officially engaged. Whether a Decision Maker begins with an open mind or a predisposition for a specific solution, as value propositioning starts and proceeds, there is always a preference once at least one solution is perceived as adequate. The preference may be for a single solution candidate, or may include multiple candidates with resolution postponed until more knowledge develops or until some tie-breaking criteria sorts out a choice from a pool of preference-indifferent candidates.

Though a Champion's value proposition has the opportunity and objective to establish a preference, it is generally not in competition on a level playing field, for it is more difficult to change an existing preference in the mind of a Decision Maker than to establish an initial preference. People have a subconscious tendency to favor reinforcement of existing beliefs over displacement of those beliefs. This does mean that the Champion who presents the first *acceptable* value proposition can develop an advantage over those that follow, if subsequent Champions cannot succeed in developing a perception of sufficient difference.

One strong source of preference development is the existing knowledge a Decision Maker brings to the process, especially with preconceived solutions. As seen earlier in the logic of group decision making, people tend to look for new solutions that are similar to other ones that they are familiar with or that they have been using but feel no longer satisfy the evolved nature of the problem.

The Agility Forum at Lehigh University in the mid-nineties shed light on this solution-dominant bias. Workshops were conducted at companies to help them design highly adaptable solutions to problems they had identified. A rigorous attempt was made to first define these problems in solution-independent terms. It was found, instead, that people defining a problem typically recognize that problem only in terms of preconceived solutions, or at least in terms of specifically desired features of a solution. Repeatedly, even after admonition and discussion, participants would phrase problem issues as lacking some feature of a favored solution, rather than needing to meet an objective. One company, for instance, was having a problem attracting development talent that restricted its growth opportunities. Participants insisted on defining the problem in terms like: "Must find ways to attract skilled engineers to move here," "Must improve local schools and training," and "Must offer better benefits to employees." These objectives were embellishments on the traditional local hiring approach. The heart of the problem was their unattractive corn-belt location, compared to the sun-belt alternatives wooing these same resources. The true objectives were to gain access to talented resources, to tap a pool of engineers experienced in their needs, to leverage their low-cost production environment with product development innovation, wherever it may be. This solution-leading tendency is deeply ingrained, and even when a benefit-based set of objectives is eventually established, it does not eliminate the thought patterns that influence solution preference. In every workshop group there were some who did not exhibit this tendency. These people were generally those who had less intimacy and history with the problem, who had given little prior thought to possible solutions, or who were uncommitted and remote from the problem personally.

A decision-making group often contains both committed and noncommitted participants. The committed usually includes those who feel personal pain with the problem, those who feel they will be directly affected by the solution, and those close to the situation who have opinions they feel need consideration. The noncommitted include people drafted for presumed expertise in the problem/solution space and people who are more concerned with the process used for evaluation and selection than with the problem or solution. Classifying them as noncommitted does not mean they do not take their participation seriously. It is a reference to their presumed indifference for the final solution beyond its choice being in conformance with their process responsibilities. For instance, a purchasing representative may be more concerned about getting the lowest possible cost and a preferential discount than in satisfying the problem. A financial representative may be more concerned with the approved method for calculating a return on investment than with contributions made by intangibles. Though the noncommitted may be indifferent initially, their special interests will also push them toward preferences that conform to these interests, under the guise of objectivity. As to the purely noncommitted technical adviser, they are rare. Whether paid consultant or internal resource, they are balancing political issues, at least subconsciously; and maintaining the reputation that brings them in as experts. As value propositioning progresses, a noncommitted Decision Maker is quite likely to behave like a committed one, though perhaps with a narrower but deeper commitment.

For a closer look at the effect of expertise, consider the example of a study done with people having mixed levels of knowledge about baseball. They were asked to choose which of three players should receive the most valuable player (MVP) award. The appropriate performance statistics for each player were provided, and the participants were reminded that 70% of the time the MVP award went to a player from the team winning the world series. Those with the most knowledge scored lower than those with less knowledge. It was suggested that those with the most knowledge made an intuitive decision, whereas those with less knowledge used a weighted-objective analytical approach independent of feelings toward the players. Notably, those with higher knowledge, but lower scores, were more confident of their choice than those with less knowledge. This effect is known as *cognitive conceit.*

This brings us finally to how biased preferences manifest themselves in decision making. Research shows that a simple personally weighted objective model appears close to how people actually arrive at preference. This says nothing about the appropriateness of the objectives and weights they choose, nor how these may change as value propositioning proceeds.

As far as the personally weighted objective model goes, there are two different models that appear to approximate what people actually do. One is known as the *linear model* and the other as the *additive difference model.* We are talking, remember, about the rolling personal preference a Decision Maker forms and evolves during the process of value propositioning, not about a formal analytical calculation done at the end to justify a choice. In form these two models look alike: a matrix with rows labeled for objectives, columns labeled for candidates, and another column that provides a weighting for each objective. This matrix is a composite mental perception, not a detailed tally record carried around and updated by the Decision Maker. The difference between the two models is in whether rows or columns predominate in the comparative scoring method. The linear model looks at a candidate column in isolation, developing some score of merit for each objective, weighting that score, and summing all to arrive at a total. In contrast, the additive difference model looks at how one candidate satisfies a particular objective in comparison to another, rolling forward a perception of preference on an objective-by-objective basis.

This later objective-centric model appears to match best the way preferences are actually formed and rolled forward. It is simpler and easier to deal with. Comparing candidates across an objective has the advantage of identical metrics. Cost is stated in monetary units, implementation time in calendar periods, and meeting threshold requirements as binary yes-or-no statements. Maintaining a perception of composite value with mixed metrics is a lot more problematic. Individual Decision Makers have favorite objectives of interest, regardless of how the official problem statement might read, and simplify their preference maintenance by focusing on these. Another common simplification: when two or more candidates end up fairly equal in the number of objectives they dominate, preference is shown for the one winning the most heavily weighted objective.

The halo effect discussed in the logic of misperception also comes into play. When people must evaluate a candidate on many objectives they appear unable to isolate these, but rather let the rat-

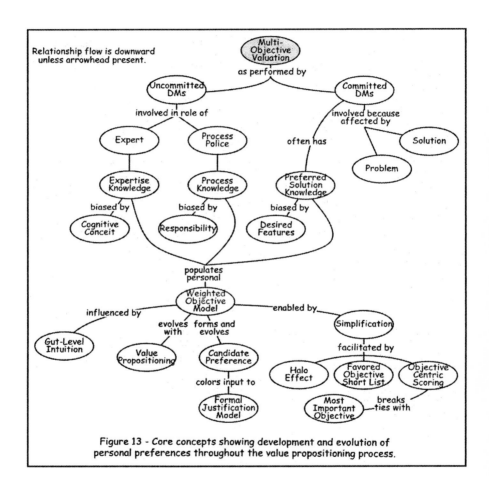

Figure 13 - Core concepts showing development and evolution of personal preferences throughout the value propositioning process.

ing they assign to one, or some, influence the ratings they give to others.

It can be seen that advantage is obtained by dominating individual value objectives over simply scoring well in all. It is possible to have the highest overall analytical score in a formal linear model, but lose the choice because preconceived preference colors the formal scoring process. The difference between an intuitive preference and what a formal scoring process may yield introduces a conflict for the Decision Maker. This conflict with the formal evaluation procedure, and the resulting confusion, is similar to the conflict and confusion introduced with standard ROI calculations, which we will discuss next.

14

Confusion with Technology and ROI

We've examined a representative range and set of psychological behaviors that influence virtually all business decisions. Now we will look specifically at the confusion factors introduced when decisions are concerned with technology, and when the decision must be supported by a return-on-investment (ROI) justification.

Though technology comes in many forms, its most common presence is in the form of digital electronic data processing and communications in a near infinite variety. The Internet has brought personal computing and email into virtually everyone's life. Home entertainment centers and cell phones escalate features yearly. Educational aids and recreational games capture the youth and insist that parents and teachers gain and maintain computer literacy. Business, wars, crime, automobiles, coffee makers, and gym equipment can't function without it. Often we can't seem to function with it. Incessant advances and increasing complexity of things in everyday life makes last year's purchases as well as last year's knowledge obsolete. Nobody wants to lose their place or become insignificant in the eyes of those who work for them, with them, or above them. Becoming insignificant, some in the field of psychology say, is a fundamental human fear. Coping occurs in a variety of ways.

Technology is awesome. No matter how little or how much we might know, it has the ability to surprise and to change the nature of life and work. I can remember the start of television, business information systems, semiconductors, satellites, moon walks, CAT scans, the Internet, cell phones, genome mapping, nanotech ... a never-ending reinforcement of the pattern. We don't need to know how it works to believe that it does. And if faith doesn't carry the day, hope will. We've seen technology deliver too often. And we've seen it fail often, too, with growing awareness in recent years. At the turn of the century, Y2K paranoia drained billions with dubious results. Surveys show that ERP implementations flounder and fail more often than not. Venture capitalists are happy with a one-in-five success rate. Power-grid failures darken major portions of the country. Security technology can't get ahead of the exploitation community. Business and technical literature is full of constant reminders that technology projects routinely fail to deliver on time, on budget, and on spec. We see powerful influences and powerful contradictions contrasting awesome faith with evident failures.

Technology also presents an emotional contradiction with the contrast of productivity and complexity. On the one hand, it empowers people with easy access to information, consolidates financial reports in a matter of hours, enables real-time performance monitoring, replaces error-prone people with robotic production lines and bank clerks with ATMs, and amplifies the engineer's command of science and accuracy. On the other hand, it meets user rejection, demands constant learning and change, refuses to integrate gracefully with existing systems, and too often triggers the costly law of unintended consequences. Decision Makers with a problem to solve or an opportunity to gain often perceive as simple that which they know well, and expect a comparably simple solution. Too often the problem perceived as simple is in fact simply perceived, however, and the ugly lessons of complex interactions etch indelible reminders. Again, we see powerful emotional influences, and powerful contradictions.

ROI is not unlike technology in presenting similar contradictions. Though it seems to be a different animal, the concept and calculation of return on investment is a technology in its own right. ROI as a prudent and necessary decision support tool is so entrenched it has taken on mythical powers. To some it is even perceived as the essence of the value proposition. Spending money in business is only justified by the expectation that the cost will be covered in a reasonable amount of time and that worthwhile profits will ensue. These financial mathematics sort out the good from the bad and set thresholds for what ought to be considered. ROI is objective. It removes the whimsical frittering away of scarce financial resources on indulgence and allure. Investing wisely is the essence of business success, and an ROI discipline ensures a wise decision will be made even when wise people are scarcer resources than money. Or so goes the myth. The flip side of this coin is the blatant abuse and condescension that routinely occurs. Typically, the ROI calculation occurs after the real decision has been made, explicitly or subconsciously, in the individual and collective minds of Decision Makers. There are many forms of ROI calculations, and many judgmental inputs to each of these calculations. When one specific way is prescribed as standard operating procedure, Decision Makers will often feel that it fails to represent the true nature of the investment value, or that it is outdated for the current business model and operating conditions. Many objectives they recognize as important they find ignored by the standard approach. They feel closest to the problem and dependent on the solution for personal performance objectives, and don't hold what they feel to be an inappropriate but prescribed ROI methodology in equal respect. It is respected, nevertheless, when sorting among acceptable alternatives, even though it is known to produce, at will, a conforming ROI calculation that can pass the necessary tests when required. All in the interest of doing what is right. Powerful influences—often subconscious—and powerful contradictions provide contrasts between myth and abuse.

ROI also presents an intellectual contradiction with its single dimension of comparison in contrast with the many methods available. As we discussed earlier, evaluating multi-objective alternatives can be very difficult. Being able to translate all objectives into a single common financial dimension has great utility and allure when trying to arrive at a composite Value for comparison. Decision Makers with serious attention-focus competition or insufficient appreciation for the nuance of benefits are especially thankful for this no-thinking-required, straightforward approach. Control is centered on sound financial management, and a variety of apples and oranges are reduced to a single metric that can not be faulted. Just as reasonably, however, one may question whether a Total Cost of Ownership model might be better than an Internal Rate of Return model for calculating ROI. Or maybe an investment in just-in-case flexible manufacturing or risk-mitigating information security might be better represented with a Real Options or Black-Scholes ROI model. But then, the Balanced Score Card methodology might better represent the intangibles necessary for future survival. Or would economic value added, rapid economic justification, or total economic impact be more appropriate at this time? If they all gave the same result it wouldn't matter, but they don't. So just how applicable is the standard process, or how arbitrary? If there isn't a standard process, which one to choose this time? Again we see powerful influences in contrast with powerful contradictions.

The behavioral aspects of perception and decision making that are ever present without this confusion are triggered and amplified with it. Contradiction triggers the cognitive-dissonance mental circuitry of misperception logic, which tends to flip the Decision Maker to one side or the other of the contradiction. Perception is polarized by a subconscious trust or distrust of technology, a reliance on or disdain for the ROI methodology. Which way the flip goes is dependent at least on current personal pressures and situations, and the current organizational political and performance contexts. Once polarized, the position has a tendency to strengthen and color expectations and hopes governing selective perception. Context dependence is influenced, with specific effects taking extra weight in conformance with hopes and expectations. Memory bias subsequently exhibits conclusions from an incomplete and self-fulfilling knowledge base.

In decision behaviors, the polarization that resolves contradiction reinforces the individual's tendency to simplify valuation and the group's preference for standard rules of valuation. A sense of contradiction alone heightens the general sense of uncertainty and can trigger uncertainty-avoidance measures in contract terms or swing favor to less aggressive and incremental solutions. One of the strongest behaviors triggered by both technology and ROI is knowledge-dependent valuation. A Decision Maker who feels knowledgeable of the technology will discount the likelihood of failure, as one well versed and experienced in the ROI methodology will trust in its usefulness. When little or no experience and knowledge are present, the opposite polarization is the more likely result.

The purpose of this discussion on confusion is to aid in its recognition, so that the Champion can engage appropriate countermeasures. Our discussion has, of course, not exhausted the many ways that confusion can occur, nor the many more ways it can cross-link into behavioral logic. Indeed, the symmetry of the accompanying concept map is the antithesis of a comprehensive picture of confusion. Symmetry does, however, amplify the visual-learning reten-

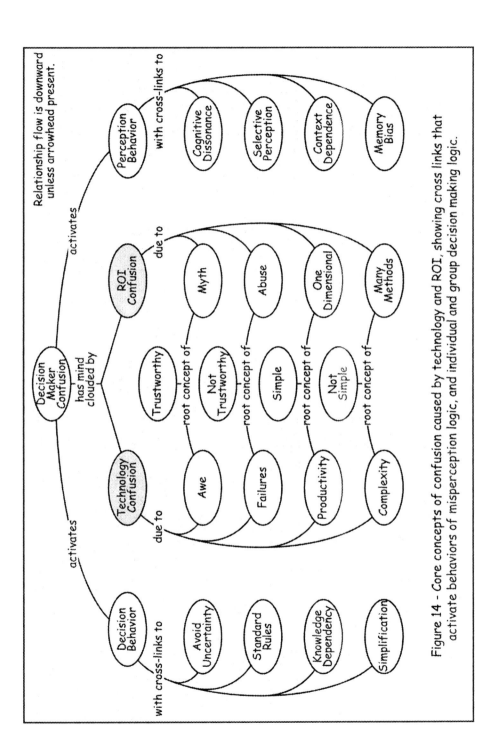

Figure 14 - Core concepts of confusion caused by technology and ROI, showing cross links that activate behaviors of misperception logic, and individual and group decision making logic.

tion featured by concept maps. The intent here is to develop a general understanding that develops an initial pattern-recognition capability—a basis of knowledge that can grow with experience, a bud of prior knowledge to which new information similar in pattern will naturally link, as learning requires in accordance with the earlier discussion on the logic of perception formation.

When confusion is evident and countermeasures are appropriate, does the large variety of triggered behaviors require an equally large variety of countermeasures? What kind of common characteristics might be found to reduce and identify the appropriate responses? The awe effect of technology and the myth effect of ROI both belong to that group of things that causes one to have trust. The contradictory concepts of technology failure and ROI abuse share an opposite root of mistrust. Similarly, the technology contrast of complexity with productivity and the ROI contrast of many methods with single dimensionality are naturally rooted in shared concepts of complexity and simplicity. From our discussion of fundamental concepts much earlier, we know that trust can be built with knowledge. From common experience we know that our perceptions of things as being complex are generally alleviated as we learn more about them, as we understand the patterns of cause and effect. Common sense even more fundamentally tells us that confusion in general is caused by a lack of knowledge.

Recognizing and identifying confusion as it occurs among Decision Makers relies on the Champion's learning skills. Educating the Decision Maker with the necessary knowledge to clear up the confusion relies on the Champion's educating skills. Again, evidence that these two skills are central to a Champion's effectiveness.

Conclusion

This first book in the Value Propositioning series has covered the fundamentals and psychological behaviors of decision making and value propositioning. It has explained how and why decision making happens the way it does. For the learner, whether Decision Maker or Decision Champion, it has pointed out the path to improvement.

The second book in this series is currently in process and will address the personal development of a Champion's competency and talent at value propositioning, consistent with the fundamentals contained in Book One. Book Three will address the same for the Decision Maker; for though value propositioning is a game played between Champion and Decision Maker, it has a win-win or lose-lose outcome.

Visit www.parshift.com/ValueProp for an update on the next book in this series, further essays on the subject, and a collaborative forum.

Want More? Now? Arm your Decision Champions and your Decision Makers with an eye-opening dose of reality. The author is available for keynotes, seminars, workshops, and meeting stimulation. Comments and inquiries are welcome via email at ValueReality@parshift.com.

References

Introduction

Niccolo Machiavelli, *The Prince*, Chapter 15, as translated by Daniel Donno, Bantam, 1984.

Chapter 5

Lewicki and Bunker, "Developing and Maintaining Trust in Work Relationships," *Trust in Organizations*, Sage Publications, pp. 114-139, 1996 [reference for three-phase trust development model].

Shapiro, Sheppard, and Cheraskin, "Business on a Handshake," *Negotiation Journal*, Vol. 8, No. 4, pp. 365-377, 1992 [reference for three-phase trust development model].

Chapter 9

Scott Plous, *The Psychology of Judgment and Decision Making*, McGraw-Hill, 1993.

Chapter 10

Nobel Prize for Daniel Kahneman, http://www.nobel.se/economics/laureates/2002/

Daniel Kahneman and Amos Tversky (Editors), *Choices, Values, and Frames*, Cambridge University Press, 2000.

Chapter 11

Nobel Prize for Herbert Simon, http://www.nobel.se/economics/laureates/1978/

Herbert Simon, *Administrative Behavior*, Free Press; 4th edition, 1997.

Richard Cyert and James March, *A Behavioral Theory of the Firm*, Blackwell Publishers, 1992.

Chapter 12

David Ausubel, *The Psychology of Meaningful Verbal Learning*, Grune & Stratton, 1963.

David Ausubel, *Educational Psychology, A Cognitive View*, International Thomson Publishing,1968.

Joseph Novak and D. Bob Gowan, *Learning How to Learn*, Cambridge University Press, 1984.

Joseph Novak, *Learning, Creating, and Using Knowledge: Concept Maps As Facilitative Tools in Schools and Corporations*, Lawrence Erlbaum Associates, 1998.

Index

perception of, 13, *See* perception

productivity. *See* confusion with technology and ROI

Prospect Theory, 49

Psychology of Judgment and Decision Making, The, 43, 87

Psychology of Meaningful Verbal Learning, The, 65, 88

real options, 81

recency effect. *See* misperception

Rhoades, Larry, vii

Ring, Jack, vii, xi, xii

risk

  as self-doubt, 22

  averse, 52

  aversion, 23

  nature of, 21

  seeking, 52

ROI, 77

  Black-Scholes, 81

  confusion with. *See* confusion with technology and ROI

  economic value added, 82

  internal rate of return, 81

  rapid economic justification, 82

  real options, 81

  total cost of ownership, 81

  total economic impact, 82

Ronayne, Mike, vii

Rynerson, Mike, vii

satisficing, 64, *See* group decision behavior

selective perception. *See* confusion with technology and ROI, *See* misperception

Shapiro, Sheppard, and Cheraskin "Business on a Handshake," 87

Simon, Herbert, xi, 57–58, 88

simple patterns. *See* group decision behavior

simplification. *See* confusion with technology and ROI

skill

  communication clarity, 32

  Decision Maker education, 32

  educating, 84

  financial, 32

  importance of, 32

  learning, 84

  modes of thinking, 33

  nature of, 32

  real-time learning, 32

  risk reduction trust building, 32

  ROI development, 32

  trade crafts, 31

slack, organizational, 60, 62, *See* group decision behavior

solution, nature of, 13

Sperat, Sergio, vii

status quo. *See* competition

strategy, real-time, 32

subjective, 3, 4, 6, 21–23, 50–51, 72

talent, nature of, 33

technology

  confusion with. *See* confusion with technology and ROI

  project failures, 25; *see also* confusion with technology and ROI

thinking modes

  competency, behavior-tuned strategy, 33

  competency, cause-and-effect logic, 33

  competency, core concepts, 32

  competency, response improvement, 33

  talent, contextual, 34

  talent, empathetic, 34

Book Two:
Talent of Champions

(A work in process, subject to change, expected publication later half of 2005)

Part 3—Strategy That Employs Skills and Conscious Practices

15.   Amateur Acts
       Purpose: To show the tactics of amateurism, common approaches that fail, and the reasons why.

16.   Preparation and Basic Knowledge Development
       Purpose: To show the nature and sources of information that develop knowledge during early engagement.

17.   Learning Skill: Listening to the Customer
       Purpose: To show the nature and value of learning skill and its practice as conceptual, logical, strategic, and responsible thinking.

18.   Educating Skill: Listening by the Customer
       Purpose: To show the nature and value of educating skill and its practice as conceptual, logical, strategic, and responsible thinking.

19.   ROI Skill: Addressing Necessity Creatively
       Purpose: To show the nature and value of ROI skill and its practice as conceptual, logical, strategic, and responsible thinking.

20.   Trust-building Skill: Reducing Uncertainty
Purpose: To show the nature and value of trust-building
(uncertainty-reducing) skill and its practice as conceptual,
logical, strategic, and responsible thinking.

21.   Communication Skill: Summarizing Effectively
Purpose: To show the nature and value of communication
skill and its practice as conceptual, logical, strategic, and
responsible thinking.

Part 4—Talent That Emerges from Skill Development

22.   Talent and Its Development
Purpose: To show the makings and making of extreme and
unconscious competency, with special attention to the
meaning and manifestation of quality.

23.   Thinking Contextually
Purpose: To show the nature and value of contextual
thinking and its emergence in the skills of learning, educating, ROI, trust building, and communication

24.   Thinking Insightfully
Purpose: To show the nature and value of insightful think-
ing and its emergence in the skills of learning, educating,
ROI, trust building, and communication.

25.   Thinking Empathetically
Purpose: To show the nature and value of empathetic
thinking and its emergence in the skills of learning, educating, ROI, trust building, and communication.

26.   Thinking Responsively
Purpose: To show the nature and value of responsive
thinking and its emergence in the skills of learning, educating, ROI, trust building, and communication.

About the Author

Rick Dove was educated as an electrical engineer at Carnegie-Mellon University, spent his early career as a systems software developer, and gravitated quickly to start-up and turnaround business management. He has run companies involved in producing software products, manufacturing machinery, manufacturing services, marketing services, management services, and fine wine production. He has led marketing and sales for companies with optical scanners, disk drives, transaction processing systems, manufacturing system-design tools, electronic postal and shipping systems, system integration services, market introduction services, and operations and strategic planning services. His consulting clients include companies such as General Motors, AT&T, Lockheed-Martin, and Hewlett-Packard. He convinced the U.S. Postal Service to approve the world's first electronic postage meter, venture capitalists to invest in innovative technology, companies to invest in all manner of products and services, national consortia to reorganize for industry leadership, and the Department of Defense to back the development of the Agile Enterprise competitive strategy. He founded and ran a company for five years that focused solely on developing market strategy and value propositions for emerging companies. He is a founder of the Agile Enterprise initiative and is respected for hands-on change management and thought leadership in all aspects of competitive business agility. He is author of *Response Ability: The Language, Structure, and Culture of the Agile Enterprise* (Wiley, 2001).

Printed in the United States
53098LVS00003B/155